M000304301

# CRYPTOCURRENCY

# CRYPTOCURRENCY

## How Digital Money Could Transform Finance

**Gian Volpicelli**

1 3 5 7 9 10 8 6 4 2

Random House Business
20 Vauxhall Bridge Road
London SW1V 2SA

Random House Business is part of the Penguin Random House
group of companies whose addresses can be found at
global.penguinrandomhouse.com.

Penguin
Random House
UK

Copyright © Gian Volpicelli, 2021

Gian Volpicelli has asserted his right to be identified as
the author of this Work in accordance with the Copyright,
Designs and Patents Act 1988.

First published by Random House Business in 2021

www.penguin.co.uk

A CIP catalogue record for this book is available from
the British Library.

ISBN 9781847943279

Typeset in 9.5/18 pt Exchange Text
by Integra Software Services Pvt. Ltd, Pondicherry

Printed and bound in Great Britain by Clays Ltd, Elcograf S.p.A.

The authorised representative in the EEA is Penguin Random House
Ireland, Morrison Chambers, 32 Nassau Street, Dublin D02 YH68.

Penguin Random House is committed to a sustainable future for
our business, our readers and our planet. This book is made from
Forest Stewardship Council® certified paper.

# Contents

# Introduction

*What is cryptocurrency?* you might ask. The question, as so often happens with questions about definitions, has multiple answers. Cryptocurrency is a thriving sector of the technology start-up scene. It is a type of digital money, a 'coin' such as Bitcoin, or Ether or Monero. Cryptocurrency can be a method to cash in on crime and malfeasance.

At its core, cryptocurrency is a technology harnessing cryptographic techniques to make it possible to exchange units of value over the internet without relying on any go-between. By using cryptocurrency, the proverbial Alice can send one unit of value to the proverbial Bob with no involvement of banks, payment companies or authorities of any kind. The integrity of that transfer is ensured by a dispersed collective of computers, none of which has the power to stop or manipulate the payment on its own.

Cryptocurrency is a challenge to the way the financial system has been working for centuries, along pipelines built and maintained by middlemen and third-party entities acting as guarantors of the honesty of transactions. It is also an attempt to facilitate the transfer of money – or money surrogates – far from the eye, and the reach, of governments. The endgame is disintermediation: the removal of as many human layers as possible from transactions and communications, keeping relationships direct and peer-to-peer. (That is, at least, the intention; the technical reality has in many cases been less than perfect.)

The answer is already, slowly, swerving from the domain of technology to that of political philosophy. And the fact is that cryptocurrency is a political programme as well as a financial one. Another of its key goals is decentralisation, or the idea that a system should not be controlled by one, or a few, actors. Decentralisation, like disintermediation, is typical of the internet age – one where politicians strive to bypass media and fact-checkers and win over voters via tweets, or where long-tail e-commerce has condemned many shops to oblivion. That is why the occasional definition of cryptocurrency as 'internet money' makes a lot of sense.

This book seeks to elaborate on these various answers by retracing cryptocurrency's steps. It will tell its history – from its origins, three decades ago, up to the latest development. It is a chronicle of the evolution of cryptocurrency, of the principles propelling it forward and of the actions of the people who invented and built it. Over five chapters, each focusing on a particular cryptocurrency era – eras, in the industry, are a matter of months – I will try and give you as detailed an answer as possible to the question: 'What is cryptocurrency – *and why should I care*?'

Gird your loins. It will be quite a ride.

# 1
# Bitcoin

---

## How crypto started

Cryptocurrency was born as a political project. That is easy to forget when most of the coverage of Bitcoin or Ethereum appears in the financial pages, on technology outlets or on specialised websites reporting on every minimal variation in the value of this or that digital coin. And it is just as hard to discern any coherent ideology at work in the mindless speculation on imaginary currencies, the preposterous peaks and troughs and the splenetic tweets of cryptocurrency evangelists.

One way to look at cryptocurrency, however, is as the endpoint of decades of experiments to bring about a technology that could undermine the very concept of government – that is, stateless digital money.

The people pursuing that goal called themselves the 'cypherpunks', a loose coalition of technologists, scholars and thinkers who first started meeting in the San Francisco Bay area in the early 1990s, and later congealed around the Cypherpunks Mailing List. Cypherpunks are what you get when digital technology becomes mixed up with libertarianism. In the cypherpunks' view, the internet was bound to become a space for freedom, autonomy, connection and the untrammelled sharing of knowledge. Threatening that idyll were governments, which would attempt to regulate the internet, use it to spy on its users and eventually rebuild it as a liberty-killing global panopticon. That was where strong cryptography came into play. Cypherpunks hoped that tools like encrypted email, anonymous networks and secure credential systems could make internet users invisible to the eyes of governments and could stave off any hint of Orwellian surveillance. In the long run, generalised use of cryptography would erode the relevance of national laws and regulations in cyberspace. Information would flow freely, and online markets selling everything from copyrighted music files to industrial secrets would mushroom all over the internet.

The ideal end-scenario was crypto-anarchy – a term coined by leading cypherpunk and Intel scientist Timothy May in a 1992 tract entitled, indeed, 'The Crypto Anarchist Manifesto'.[1] As May explained in a later, longer article,[2] crypto-anarchy involved the collapse of government and the advent of a political order with 'no outside rulers and laws. Voluntary arrangements, back-stopped by voluntarily-arranged institutions [...] will be the only form of rule.' The 'crypto' in 'crypto-anarchy' was both a wink at political slurs like 'crypto-fascist' and a serious acknowledgement of the role cryptography would play in triggering a welcome shift to 'a system which will develop as cyberspace becomes more important. A system which dispenses with national boundaries, which is based on voluntary (even if anonymous) free trade. At issue is the end of governments as we know them today.' No borders, no taxes, no laws.

Not all cypherpunks have been as ardently anti-government as May, a radical ideologue whose political parable would eventually land in far-right territory. But at a bare minimum, most of the mailing list's 700-plus subscribers – among them British businessman Adam Back, free-software theorist Richard Stallman and future WikiLeaks founder Julian Assange[3] – deemed privacy desirable, surveillance dangerous and dreamed of an internet free from any governmental oversight.

By the time cypherpunks started outlining their vision, some of its pieces were already falling into place. PGP (Pretty Good Privacy), a program that could be used to encrypt online communications, had been launched in 1991. Anonymous remailers – systems that rerouted emails to their intended recipients while keeping the sender secret – were catching on, adding further layers of anonymity. One thing remained elusive, and that was anonymous digital cash.

The cypherpunk libertarian endgame could not dispense with libertarianism's lynchpin, the free market.

In May's view, cyberspace was not only to become a forum for unimpeded anonymous communication, but also an emporium, where all sorts of goods, services and information – licit and, especially, illicit – could be traded.[4] That posed the problem of what currency those transactions should be done in. Electronic payment systems like those provided by banks or credit-card companies were obviously not an option: they required payer and payee to use their real names, a requirement that was at odds with cypherpunks' veneration of anonymity. More seriously, they left behind records that could be subpoenaed by governments for the purpose of surveillance or, in the case of illegal trade, prosecution. As another founding cypherpunk, Eric Hughes, wrote in 'A Cypherpunk Manifesto', an essay published online in 1993, 'privacy in an open society requires anonymous transaction systems'.[5] Ordinarily, Hughes added, that function is performed by cash.

But cash was deemed to be bad too, for a myriad of reasons. Some were material: it would be absurd to power cyberspace-based anonymous markets with wads of banknotes sent through the post or – worse – handed over in risky face-to-face meetings. Others were conceptual: even if not all cypherpunks longed for the outright disappearance of government, many of them subscribed to the ideas of the Austrian School of economics,[6] which came of age in Vienna in the late nineteenth and early twentieth centuries and included Margaret Thatcher's fetish thinker Friedrich von Hayek. Its members decried the existence of government-issued currency, believing that money should have some kind of stable and intrinsic value, the way gold and silver do. When it does not (as is the case with modern currencies, whose value derives from a government's say-so rather than from their convertibility into precious metal), the Austrians feared that the central bank's policy would arbitrarily increase or diminish the currency's value and, in so doing, damage creditors with inflation and debtors with deflation. One way out of this predicament, Hayek had argued in his book *The Denationalisation of Money,*[7] would be for private citizens and organisations to issue their own currencies in competition among themselves and with the government's legal tender, and let users decide which one to trade in. That would, Hayek's argument went, result in the prevalence of the fittest monies, those whose value was not debased by a government's inflationary whims.

What cypherpunks needed, then, was something other than cash, or bank-issued electronic currency. Something *new*, which combined the anonymity of a banknote with the speediness and global reach of electronic money transfers – and possibly with the stability the Austrians yearned for. That was not easy.

The first challenge to inventing such a currency is known as the double-spending problem. If you are trying to create a digital unit of currency, you will likely end up with something akin to a file, possibly featuring a string of characters as a unique identifier – the way notes are marked with serial numbers. But notes are made of atoms, while our hypothetical digital note will be made of bits, and that poses a problem. While a paper note is unequivocally spent the moment it changes hands – you either have a $10 bill or you don't – a file can be sent multiple times to multiple payees. A dishonest digital-cash user could decide just to spend the same unit of currency over and over again – namely, double-spend it. That is an existential threat to any attempt to build a payment system worth its salt. The most straightforward way of solving it is by having a third-party arbiter keep track of the transactions, clearing those that are legitimate and nixing those involving money that has been spent by the same payer more than once.[8] It is essentially what banks do.

But that raised another issue: centralisation. Placing an arbiter or bank at the centre of a payment network not only ran counter to the cypherpunks' crypto-anarchist ethos, but also created what computer scientists call a 'single point of failure' – something too crucial to a system's existence for its own good. Central authorities can be hacked, captured by hostile players or simply browbeaten by governments into blocking transactions that involve certain goods – drugs and guns, sure, but also banned books in Saudi Arabia or China – thus fatally undermining May's free-market utopia. A solution to this is to entrust the functioning of the system not to one party, but to a larger, open-to-join network of independent referees.[9] In this decentralised model, the referees keep track of the amount of digital cash owned by every user, and wave legitimate transactions through – and block those that would plunge a payer's balance into the red.

This in turn, however, raises another problem. In cyberspace – or at least, in the cypherpunk version of it – everyone is anonymous, and you cannot check the identity of the referees. That makes it impossible to tell whether an attacker is running an army of sock puppets to accrue the majority necessary to approve payments that should not be approved and is thus wreaking havoc on the system's credibility. Avoiding that requires a tantalising contortion: you want the referee network to remain open to join, in order to increase decentralisation and make it harder for the authorities to attack the system; you also want people partaking in the system to have some financial skin in the game, so that no criminal or governmental agency would be able simply to pile in people to distort its functioning; still, it cannot be too expensive, or at least it has to come with some incentives, otherwise no one would ever volunteer to be a referee. The question is: can this delicate balance be achieved?

From the mid-1980s onwards, the cypherpunks grappled with these – and sundry other – problems. Piece by piece, they inched closer to the solution. Cryptographer David Chaum (regarded as the forefather of the cypherpunks, although he wasn't a mailing-list subscriber), and cypherpunks Adam Back, Nick Szabo, Hal Finney (a key PGP developer) and Wei Dai, all added to the conversation about how to create digital cash – also known as cryptocurrency, given that its inviolability would be guaranteed by cryptography. In some cases their ideas remained on paper; in others, they evolved into real-world projects and even companies, albeit short-lived ones. But none of them would turn out to be the tipping point that sent digital cash mainstream. That changed in 2008.

# The White Paper

One of the most influential pieces of writing in the history of the internet appeared on Halloween 2008, as the world was still reeling from the explosion of the subprime mortgage crisis.

'I've been working on a new electronic cash system that's fully peer-to-peer, with no trusted third party,' read an email sent to the Cryptography Mailing List, which counted several original cypherpunks among its subscribers. (Full paper at http://www.bitcoin.org/bitcoin.pdf) The email was signed 'Satoshi Nakamoto'.

Satoshi Nakamoto was a pseudonym. Despite journalistic efforts, internet investigations and the appearance of pretenders to Nakamoto's throne, the real identity of the person, or people, behind the moniker remains a mystery. Today, years after he or she last wrote a line, Nakamoto has graduated to the status of internet legend, or even internet prophet, so much so that in 2020 an article in the *Atlantic* magazine[10] compared Nakamoto to John Titor – a *soi-disant* time-traveller whose apocalyptic predictions garnered a sizeable online following in the early 2000s – and to Q, the worryingly popular internet conspiracist behind QAnon. But there is a difference between those pseudonymous figures and Satoshi Nakamoto: John Titor and QAnon are fabulists whose claim to fame is a knack for spinning fantastical tales able to captivate their followers' imagination (and, in QAnon's case, push them to commit violence); Satoshi Nakamoto is an inventor, whose legacy is a very concrete tool – albeit one promoting a narrative about what the internet and money should be. If we were to ride with the prophetic analogy, Titor and QAnon are two small-time cult leaders, whereas Nakamoto is Moses, handing the Tablets of the Law to cypherpunks who had long been waiting for the advent of digital cash. Those tablets were the so-called Bitcoin White Paper.[11]

The nine-page-long document that Nakamoto sent to the Cryptography Mailing List was entitled 'Bitcoin: A Peer-to-Peer Electronic Cash System', and was a technical but pithy roadmap to create stateless internet money. Nakamoto clearly knew cryptography and had read the work of key cypherpunks (references included Adam Back and Wei Dai). So what was his or her plan? What is Bitcoin?

Bitcoin is the name of Nakamoto's proposed digital-payment network, of the digital cash exchanged on it and the software that makes that possible; later on, the word would sometimes be used as a shorthand for cryptocurrency in general, or to define a particular mindset about the technology's potential, as in the formula 'Bitcoin maximalist'.

Let's stick to the first meaning, and start with a trite but effective simile: think of Bitcoin as email for money. Not just any ordinary email, though, but something called public-key cryptography email: a kind of email affording stronger privacy. To transmit an email in this way, the sender needs two long numeric codes: the first, which they need to keep secret to avoid hacks and impersonations, is their 'private key' – a password they can use to sign a message in an unforgeable way and prove that they authored it; the second is the recipient's 'public key': a digital padlock that everyone can use to conceal from others the content of emails sent to that specific recipient, and which can only be unlocked by the recipient's own private key. Nakamoto's project works in a similar way. The owner of a certain amount of digital cash – bitcoin – needs a private key in order to spend it, and the payee's public key (in fact, more often a shortened version of it) in order to transfer the sum to that person's balance. These movements are generally managed through a device, software or app called a 'wallet', which contains a user's public and private keys.

In keeping with cypherpunk norms, anyone can use Bitcoin without revealing their identity – even if that has become harder over time. On the other hand, all payments happen in the open: anyone can see how much a certain anonymous wallet has paid to another anonymous wallet. That is probably where the Bitcoin-as-email narrative breaks down. Unlike emails, bitcoins are not *sent* from payer to payee. Rather, a payer creates a 'transaction'. This is a stack of data that in Nakamoto's design – things have evolved since – includes information about payer and payee, the amount of bitcoin changing hands and a code referencing the transaction in which the payer received that amount (a sort of digital title deed). Transactions are publicly broadcast to a network of referees, like the one cypherpunks had floated as a way to prevent double-spending without enthroning a centralised authority. In Bitcoin's case, there is a swarm of computers running the Bitcoin software, called 'nodes'. Anyone with a laptop, an internet connection and an interest in cryptocurrency can set up a node. Each node maintains an identical copy of an online ledger detailing all the Bitcoin transactions that ever took place on the network – a chain of ownerships showing how much bitcoin each user possessed at any given time. When a new transaction is announced, it ripples through the network, as node after node checks against the ledger whether the payer owns the bitcoins they are spending. If so, the transaction is cleared to go through – but is not confirmed yet.

Confirming those transactions and etching the changes of ownership in the ledger is the job of a specific subset of nodes, called 'mining nodes' or 'miners'. The word appears just once in the White Paper, as a metaphor for the people running nodes, which according to Nakamoto are 'analogous to gold miners expending resources to add gold to circulation'. To understand that, think back to the problem that cypherpunks had pondered when considering a decentralised refereeing structure as opposed to a sole intermediary. You want to keep access to the network of referees as open as possible: the more nodes on the Bitcoin network, the harder for a government to target one of them and block transactions. But if joining the network is too easy, then malicious parties might hijack the system.

Hence Nakamoto's decision that confirming transactions should be costly. Miners have to gather hundreds of valid transactions in bundles – called 'blocks' – and vie with one another to append them to the ledger. In order to earn that privilege, a miner has to solve a mathematical puzzle based on a hash function. That is an algorithm that can convert any chunk of data – from 'Hello, world' to the whole *The Lord of the Rings* trilogy – into a hash, or string of digits, of a standard size. Hashes are popular in cryptography because, while parlaying data into a hash is easy, reverse-engineering the data by looking at the hash is nigh-on impossible. Bitcoin miners are supposed to transform the block's transaction data into a 256-bit hash, with the extra criterion – and here's the puzzle – that it start with a certain number of zeros. To meet that condition, miners add an extra number (called 'nonce') to the transaction data, in the hope that it will return the right result. How do they find it? Guesswork. A mining node automatically tries out random numbers in rapid succession until it stumbles upon the solution.

Doing all that takes powerful computers and electricity to power them. That is why Nakamoto said that miners were 'expending resources', and why this system is called 'proof-of-work'. Of course the people running mining nodes are not burning through cash out of altruism: there is a prize to be won. The mining node that first cracks the puzzle immediately notifies its fellow miners – which check whether the block contains valid transactions and, if so, update their ledgers accordingly. Nodes do the same, and the ledger is updated across the network. The winning miner is rewarded with a certain number of bitcoins: the 'gold' in Nakamoto's metaphor. That reward halves every four years – a feature dubbed 'the halvening' – as Nakamoto established that the bitcoin stock should be finite: 21 million. Miners can also receive small Bitcoin fees from users who want their transactions to be processed more swiftly. (Once the last block is mined, circa 2140, the miners' incentive will consist entirely of transaction fees.) That is one testament to how Nakamoto's code is steeped in politics.

Bitcoin is conceived in the spirit of the Austrian School: it flirts with the gold standard, denationalises money and – crucially – enshrines an automatic money-spewing algorithm where usually there is a central bank able to increase or decrease the money stock.

'The root problem with conventional currency is all the trust that's required to make it work. The central bank must be trusted not to debase the currency, but the history of fiat currencies is full of breaches of that trust,' Nakamoto wrote in a post[12] on the P2P Foundation forum in early 2009, portending how 'trust' would be central to cryptocurrency debates. Such pontifications were sporadic, however. In a message to the Cryptography Mailing List, Nakamoto quipped, '[Bitcoin is] very attractive to the libertarian viewpoint if we can explain it properly. I'm better with code than with words though.'[13]

But the code – while razor-sharp in its ideological clarity – is also utilitarian and prone to compromises. Jaya Klara Brekke, an assistant professor researching decentralised technology at the University of Durham, points out[14] that while Bitcoin's mining implies a 'commodity theory of money' – money is something with intrinsic value, like gold – the system's ledger element, in which one's possessions exist as entries in the network's global balance sheet, gestures towards an opposite take, which Brekke calls 'the credit theory of money'.

And the code evolves. Take mining. The White Paper makes no distinction between nodes and miners: all nodes mine. Today, most nodes do not mine – they simply keep a copy of the ledger, relay transactions and add robustness. That is because the mathematical puzzle that miners have to crack gets harder over time, and solving it grows costlier. In the early days, amateurs could mine from a laptop; nowadays, mining is a business, performed by battalions of hyper-specialised servers delocalised to countries where electricity is cheap. That is just one example of how, while adherence to 'Satoshi's vision' would later grow into a fetish, the rules of Bitcoin have been debated, upgraded and changed several times since Halloween 2008.

That tension is inevitable, though. Bitcoin has had to evolve. But at the same time the idea of immutability is baked in the system, starting from its backbone, the ledger – also known, of course, as the 'blockchain'.[15] In the White Paper, Nakamoto simply called it 'chain', the reason being that every block that is mined, validated by a majority of miners and nodes and added to the ledger is inextricably linked to the previous block, like a metal link is to another link. In the same way that a transaction's data refer to the transaction in which the payer had received that Bitcoin amount, every block contains a cryptographic reference to the previous block – and so forth, back to the first block ever mined.

That architecture prevents attackers from changing past transactions and opening the door to double-spending. Anyone trying to manipulate an old transaction would have to re-mine not only the block containing the transaction, but also all the blocks that follow it, whose data reference the hacked block. That is no mean feat: mining a block takes on average ten minutes; when the attacker attempts to re-mine one block, the other miners will have likely added one new block to the blockchain. Every ten minutes, as the attacker scrambles to modify all the blocks needed to rewrite history, a new mined block pops up, complicating those efforts. For that mechanism to work, however, Nakamoto established one condition in the code: mining nodes should always attach new blocks to the longest chain. Otherwise hackers could simply re-mine the block they want to change and trick other miners into following them on the shorter, doctored chain. (Hackers might also try to disrupt the ledger by deploying enough computing power to take over the majority of mining nodes – a scenario known as '51% attack' – but proof-of-work should make that kind of attack too onerous and the pay-off relatively small.) Everything in Nakamoto's project was aimed at ensuring that transactions cannot be blocked, censored or reversed – an arguable downside for the victims of scams, but a thumping victory for the cypherpunks.

What gave Bitcoin its value? Unlike the dollar pre-1971, its value was not backed by gold; also unlike the dollar post-1971, Bitcoin's value was not guaranteed by a government's say-so and its consequent acceptability as a medium for paying taxes. From a literal point of view, Bitcoin's value today is the result of the meeting of demand and supply on online exchanges, where Bitcoin is sold for government-issued currency. Each exchange will set a different dollar-denominated price, depending on average trading volumes on its platform. This is why, while Bitcoin's price is generally in the same ballpark across all platforms, traders enjoy some room for arbitrage between different exchanges.

This technical explanation, however, does not answer why people might want to pay for Bitcoin. The debate on this point is heated and is still evolving, given how Bitcoin and the way it is used have been changing since its debut. But one online post that Nakamoto wrote in 2010 gives us some sense of what he or she might think Bitcoin's value was. In the post,[16] Nakamoto posited the existence of a rare metal that was dull and useless in all respects, except for a single property: it could easily be transmitted from one person to another. He went on to argue that 'If [this metal] somehow acquired any value at all for whatever reason, then anyone wanting to transfer wealth over a long distance could buy some, transmit it, and have the recipient sell it. Maybe it could get an initial value circularly as you've suggested, by people foreseeing its potential usefulness for exchange.'

In other words: it was all about Bitcoin's properties. In the same way that the choice of gold as a medium of exchange was rooted in the metal's rarity, shininess, malleability and resistance to corrosion, among other things, so Bitcoin's value supposedly derived from its ability to be transferred with no risk of being blocked or reversed. In that reading, as long as there are people who find that useful – whether for libertarian yearning, criminal intent or anti-surveillance purposes – Bitcoin will have some kind of value; speculation will take care of the rest.

# Taking off

Initial reactions to the White Paper were all pieces of criticism, poking holes in various aspects of Nakamoto's proposal. Nakamoto patiently addressed all of them, and as the conversation went on, the excitement among members of the Cryptography Mailing List became palpable. The mailing list was taken over by Bitcoin talks, to the point that on 17 November 2008, Admin. Perry E. Metzger sent a message[17] entitled 'end of bitcoin discussion for now', asking that the budding Bitcoin community continue its conversation elsewhere. So it did: first on another mailing list, then on a dedicated forum – Bitcointalk – which Nakamoto set up in November 2009. Over hundreds of emails, forum posts and private messages, Bitcoin went from technical manifesto to vibrant open-source project. On 3 January 2009 the Bitcoin network was launched: Nakamoto mined the first block ever and, as a further time-stamp, added a brief comment to the block: 'The Times 03/Jan/2009 Chancellor on brink of second bailout for banks'. That was a real headline from London's *The Times*, detailing Chancellor of the Exchequer Alistair Darling's plans to save the ailing Lloyds and Royal Bank of Scotland. Bitcoin entered the world with a barb against banks and government spending.

Bitcoin's ensuing success – even the most spiteful critics of the project would recognise that it has ultimately brought the idea of digital cash into the mainstream – was first of all due to Satoshi Nakamoto's ability to leverage existing technology in order to attain the cypherpunk vision. There was also something else at play: in 2008 Bitcoin seemed a technology whose time had come – a tool that chimed with the zeitgeist. At its core, Bitcoin's promise was disintermediation: the elimination of 'middlemen' in favour of direct exchanges between peers. The idea of disintermediation had first emerged among economists in the 1960s, to describe a trend of decreasing reliance on financial intermediaries such as commercial banks and pension funds. But with the rise of the internet, the term acquired an all-encompassing, disruptive connotation as a phenomenon that could affect many industries. Disintermediation became a watchword of the dot-com bubble era, and would find a concrete realisation after the bubble burst in the 2000s. By the time of Nakamoto's announcement, a lot of people – not only cypherpunks – had been primed to *get* what Bitcoin was about. They had seen how the internet had made traditional travel agencies superfluous as channels to buy plane tickets or book hotels; how e-commerce had allowed manufacturer and buyer to trade directly, cutting out wholesaler and retailer; and even how social networks were enabling politicians and public figures to bypass the media to connect with their audiences. Bitcoin promised to do the same for money: no payment companies, no financial institutions, no central banks – only mathematical code. That aspiration to remove extra layers of intermediation – regarded as either useless rent-seekers or security liabilities – would define most cryptocurrency projects from Bitcoin onwards.[18]

Still, Bitcoin's penetration into the mainstream was gradual: as of mid-2010, one bitcoin was priced at less than $0.1 on the few exchanges already in existence. That spell of obscurity would not last. 'One important milestone in Bitcoin's history was WikiLeaks,' says Klara Jaya Brekke of Durham University. In November 2010, when the whistleblowing venture built by former Cypherpunks subscriber Julian Assange was blacklisted and rendered unable to raise funds through conventional payment platforms, the Bitcointalk crowd started discussing whether they should advise Assange to accept Bitcoin donations. After all, wasn't this a textbook Bitcoin use case – countering state-sponsored censorship of payments? Nakamoto, still active on the forum at the time, strongly opposed the idea, wary of 'the heat' that the association with WikiLeaks would bring upon Bitcoin. People came round and did not contact WikiLeaks. But soon journalists stumbled upon the story – and articles appeared online making the case that, at least in theory, Bitcoin might provide a solution for WikiLeaks's predicament.[19] As one Bitcointalk user quipped, 'the genie is out of the bottle'. Nakamoto's take was similar: 'WikiLeaks has kicked the hornet's nest, and the swarm is headed towards us,' he or she wrote on 11 December 2010, one day after the initial press reports about Bitcoin and WikiLeaks. Nakamoto would write only one other post, one day later, and then stopped writing on the forum. In an email exchange with a senior Bitcoin developer, Nakamoto explained having 'moved on to other things'. In June 2011 WikiLeaks started accepting Bitcoin.[20]

It wasn't just the aftershock of the WikiLeaks affair that made 2011 a pivotal year for Bitcoin. In the first place, it saw the arrival of imitations: developers used Bitcoin as a blueprint to create new forms of digital cash – sometimes dubbed 'altcoins' – adding new features. Namecoin and Litecoin, two prominent examples, were both launched in 2011. Almost as if following Friedrich von Hayek's doctrine, the space had started to morph into a competition among several cryptocurrencies. This was also the year that Vitalik Buterin, a 17-year-old

Russian-Canadian programmer, became enamoured with the idea of Bitcoin – and started working on the launch of a specialist publication, *Bitcoin Magazine*. Two years later Buterin would be instrumental in the creation of another cryptocurrency – Ethereum – which, as we will see, triggered a change of paradigm across the whole scene. And 2011 was the year when Texas-born libertarian Ross Ulbricht launched Silk Road – an online marketplace for illegal drugs, which existed on the dark web and used Bitcoin as a form of payment. The crypto-anarchist utopia envisioned by Timothy May had finally come to pass – and in the process Bitcoin had earned the shady label of criminal currency that it is still struggling to shake off a decade later.

If Silk Road might have popularised Bitcoin among a new crowd (the drug-buying one), it was Silk Road's highly publicised demise in October 2013 that arguably helped Bitcoin usage to spike worldwide. An analysis[21] of Bitcoin price variations on online exchanges between 2012 and 2018, published by the Royal Society in 2019, suggests that Ulbricht's arrest might have been one of the factors behind a major Bitcoin bubble that took off in the second half of 2013, which peaked on 4 December, when one bitcoin was valued at $1,132. 'The closure of Silk Road symbolically set free Bitcoin as a proper investment for more cautious investors who, until then, were deterred by its illegal usage as drug money,' the article reads. Several other factors were at play here – from the Eurozone debt crisis, which had resulted in many Europeans looking for a store of value beyond the purview of government, to the increasing interest that Bitcoin was arousing in China. And many other bubbles would follow: the article lists 13 – the most explosive of which, in 2017, would bring Bitcoin's price to $19,783.06 per unit. Those bubbles have deflated, but certainly not burst altogether: as of July 2020, the value of all Bitcoin in the world was estimated to be around $118 billion. In a way, the fall of Silk Road was the swansong of Bitcoin as a currency, and the kick-off of the era of Bitcoin as a speculative investment,[22] which is still prevalent today. (Even if that might be changing again after electric vehicle company Tesla announced it would accept Bitcoin payments, in early 2021.)

# Unfinished business

By the time of its 2013 explosion, Bitcoin existed in a world very different from the one in which it had appeared in 2008. Nakamoto's brainchild had materialised in a technical void: it was the only cryptocurrency in existence. Fast-forward four years, and 'cryptocurrency' was a word often declined in the plural – given the arrival of a swarm of digital cash projects inspired, one way or another, by the Bitcoin example. To some extent, from that point on most of the innovation – but also most of the degeneration, the hucksterism, the hare-brained schemes – in the field would take place in projects other than Bitcoin. If anything, that is because the Bitcoin community is so strongly attached to its scripture – the White Paper – that any deviation from it is bound to provoke furious arguments and the occasional schism. And if, on the one hand, several second-wave cryptocurrency frameworks integrate, or hearken back to Bitcoin in some way, on the other hand the Bitcoin community has witnessed the rise of a vocal tribe of 'Bitcoin maximalists', who dismiss every coin other than Bitcoin as either unsound or a scam.

That is not to say that the Bitcoin community is monolithic or fossilised. Quite the contrary: Bitcoin's prominence has forced the community – to wit: the developers, the miners, the people running nodes, the exchanges and high-profile social-media commentators – to come to grips with several issues that, if left unaddressed, have the potential to undermine the project's long-term success.

Maybe the most fundamental has to do with what Bitcoin should be. The Bitcoin-as-money v. Bitcoin-as-investment dichotomy is not academic: it has very technical implications. If Bitcoin is investment, it is something to buy and stash away, like gold bullion. If Bitcoin is money, its competitors are payment companies like Visa. Visa claims to have the capacity to process

56,000 transactions per second; as of 2020, Bitcoin can handle seven – too slow for a decent payment network.[23] Part of the reason for this has to do with the blocks constituting the blockchain: Nakamoto designed them to have a maximum size of 1MB, so limiting the amount of transactions each block can pack, and which can be added to the ledger within the customary ten minutes. That is why the debate on Bitcoin scalability often revolves around making blocks bigger – a solution that comes with its own problems, given that bigger blocks would take up more space on a machine's hard disk, a fact that would in turn make it more expensive to run a node, (further) concentrating power in the hands of a few miners. In 2017 that dispute resulted in a showdown between advocates of bigger blocks – mostly Asian miners, captained by Roger Ver a.k.a. 'Bitcoin Jesus', an ultra-libertarian who in 2005 served ten months in prison for selling explosives on eBay, and later renounced his American citizenship – and the proponents of SegWit (Segregated Witness), a software solution that would allow the cramming of more transactions into the blocks without expanding their size. In August 2017 the Ver-led crowd went its own way, splitting (or 'forking') the chain to launch an alternative version of Bitcoin – Bitcoin Cash, able to process up to 116 transactions per second. 'That split reflected two different visions of Bitcoin's nature,' says Brekke. Other forks would follow.

Crucial to many of those ideological standoffs has been the subject of decentralisation. One of the declared pillars of the Bitcoin ethos – its robustness – has come under increasing scrutiny as mining has evolved into a corporate business. As of early 2020,[24] 49.9 per cent of the network's mining went through five mining ventures – all of them China-based mining 'pools', which enable small miners to join forces and then divvy up the proceeds. That concentration of power is a red flag for lovers of decentralisation, and one suggesting that all the talk about decentralisation in Bitcoin circles might be just spin, hiding the usual power structures. 'Decentralisation tends to be much more of a marketing, or an aspirational term than something that is actually descriptive of the systems [in the cryptocurrency sector],' says Angela Walch, a professor of law at St Mary's University in San Antonio, Texas. 'I think it's a kind of a cover for people who want to act like they don't have power.' On the other hand, the Bitcoin community is made up of several groups, which in a way have a countervailing influence on each other. Miners are powerful, but so are those running non-mining full nodes, and so are the developers who maintain github.com/Bitcoin/Bitcoin, the repository containing Bitcoin's code.

'In Bitcoin, there are influences and political dynamics similar to any open-source project,' says Andrew Miller, an assistant professor at the University of Illinois and a board member of several cryptocurrency ventures. 'There's some tendency to want to deny that there's such a social or political structure that's making all of that work. They'll say things like, "This has to be this way because it's backed by mathematics". And all of that is nonsense. It really is just a social consensus process.'

Another key issue is anonymity. The cypherpunks dreamed of anonymous digital cash, but Bitcoin has never been completely anonymous: transactions are all publicly broadcast, and one single revealing mistake can end up unmasking who hides behind a certain address. For instance, if a suspect has ever moved funds through a custodial wallet – one whose cryptographic keys are held by third-party companies like exchanges, which often carry out identity checks on their users – the chance that they will be tracked down is very high. That is made even more likely by the emergence of security companies like Chainalysis or Elliptic, which deploy machine-learning techniques to connect wallets to personal information. More privacy- and anonymity-focused cryptocurrencies have emerged in the last few years, including Monero, Zcash and Grin.

There's also an environmental question, which is Bitcoin's original sin: Bitcoin mining consumes as much electricity in one year as Sweden. In a world besieged by climate change, how moral is an enterprise whose functioning hinges on proof-of-work – that is, on wasting humongous amounts of energy 'just because'? For that reason, most of the new cryptocurrency projects have usually made a point of dispensing with proof-of-work altogether – or having a roadmap to eventually do away with it. But that story goes well beyond Bitcoin.

## 2

# Ethereum

## Into the ether

Bitcoin is about money. Satoshi Nakamoto designed it as a system to move units of value from one person to another without relying on intermediaries. But almost immediately after its launch, developers and enthusiasts started looking for ways of using the Bitcoin blockchain for applications other than currency.

At the most basic level, that meant adding comments to a transaction – the way Nakamoto had attached *The Times*'s headline to the genesis block – to send each other uncensorable, albeit public, messages. That could turn ugly: a 2018 study found that on-blockchain comments were littered with hundreds of links to child pornography images.[1]

But most of the proposed 'Bitcoin 2.0' uses were less seedy, and more creative. In 2011 a project called NameCoin emerged, proposing to leverage the Bitcoin network to create a decentralised Domain Name System. In 2012 developers floated the concept of 'coloured coins': small amounts of Bitcoin ('satoshis', equivalent to one one-hundred-millionth of a bitcoin) tagged in distinct ways and considered easily tradable stand-ins for assets like bonds, gold bullion or land property deeds.

Those ideas flew in the face of the fact that Bitcoin was a one-trick pony, struggling with scalability problems, and constantly undergoing tweaks as its community grew bigger. Any project built on top of its infrastructure risked being jeopardised by those changes: when Bitcoin introduced a minimum transaction amount of 5,430 satoshis, in April 2013, coloured-coin advocates decried that as a setback.

A possible way out of that pickle would be for each project to launch its own function-specific blockchain and coin. The problem with that approach was that in a world overcrowded with thousands of blockchains, interoperability would be far from guaranteed: each chain risked becoming a small crypto-island, with its standards, its coin and no obvious way to take advantage of synergies with other similar blockchains. Irrelevance beckoned. The alternative was to reject fragmentation and instead create a single blockchain designed in such a way that other projects – and other coins – could be built on top of it. Among the exponents of the latter approach was Vitalik Buterin.

Buterin had come a long way since his discovery of Bitcoin as a 17-year-old in 2011. His nerves were still raw from quitting the online multi-player game *World of Warcraft* after the game developer had suddenly yanked a special ability from his character – an experience that, Buterin says, made him realise 'what horrors centralized services can bring'.[2] Buterin was initially sceptical of Nakamoto's idea, but wound up being won over by it. Along-side someone he met online, he started *Bitcoin Magazine* and became the outlet's top writer. His first article was about why teenagers – like him – should use Bitcoin.[3]

Wisely, Buterin was not planning for a career as a trade journalist. A gifted programmer, lover of economics and future recipient of a fellowship bankrolled by Silicon Valley's grandee Peter Thiel, Buterin used *Bitcoin Magazine* as a listening post to get involved in cryptocurrency projects, and as a platform to promulgate his ideas about the scene. By 2013 he had grown convinced that the sector was stuck in a bad routine: everyone was attempting to graft functions onto Bitcoin that it was not intended to perform. Developers were scrambling to run online apps on top of what, at its core, was an email-like protocol. To create something more complex than an email system – something akin to online services and Internet-connected applications – you needed a platform that behaved like the Internet. Buterin thought he could program that decentralised internet; in a White Paper he published in late 2013, he called it Ethereum.

Ethereum's grand unveiling came in January 2014, at the North American Bitcoin Conference in Miami, where Buterin expounded his vision in a 28-minute-long pitch. It was immediately clear that he would become a charismatic figure: ridiculously young but extraordinarily self-assured on technical matters; apt at deploying metaphors and at cracking offbeat jokes; awkward in his delivery – with the occasional fluff and the frequent verbal tic – yet mesmerising. Tall and skeletal, with piercing blue eyes locked in a perpetual thousand-yard stare, Vitalik Buterin was the geek's idea of a messiah, baby Jesus with a command line. All the lore that would grow up around him over the following years – his IQ is 257, he has learned Mandarin in two months, he is an alien – started accreting the moment he concluded his Miami talk, to thunderous applause.

What Buterin was proposing was a Bitcoin with consequences. If a Bitcoin transaction resembled a person handing a coin to another person, an Ethereum transaction was supposed to be akin to inserting a coin in a vending machine and immediately getting a cup of smoking-hot coffee in the tray. Where Bitcoin's network made sure that no one could stop or reverse money changing hands,

Ethereum could go a step further, ensuring that a payment resulted in the payer's expected outcome – that is, the delivery of the digital equivalent of a cup of coffee.

The Ethereum blockchain, which would eventually go live in July 2015, has been designed to support two types of accounts: standard Bitcoin-like addresses where users can send and receive Ethereum's cryptocurrency, called Ether; and contract accounts – unmanned addresses that behave like vending machines. Contract accounts are predicated on the concept of 'smart contract', an idea floated by first-wave cypherpunk Nick Szabo[4] in a 1996 essay, which explored how digital technology allowed the creation of financial covenants whose enforcement did not depend on lawyers or mediators, but was inescapably etched in computer code.

Sending a payment – or any other input, like a message – to an Ethereum contract account automatically triggers the execution of its code. A contract could, for instance, be programmed to immediately issue a digital token representing a property title (*à la* coloured coins) to anyone paying it with Ether. Or it might act as an escrow between two parties, safely stowing ethers until the payer receives a purchase and gives the go-ahead to forward the sum to the payee. Or again, a contract might be designed to receive weather reports from an external feed – dubbed 'oracle' – and automatically pay an insurance premium to farmers who are likely to suffer a loss because of scorching heat or torrential rains. Buterin characterised Ethereum as 'Turing complete',[5] meaning that smart contracts can be engineered to carry out virtually every conceivable operation, through the combination of a large number of different instructions (as of August 2020, there are 142 instructions, or 'opcodes'). Anyone can create a contract account on Ethereum by enshrining the contract's source code into the network via a transaction.

According to Ethereum's architects, the advantage of smart contracts is that they not only allow for more complex operations to be carried out – instead of jury-rigging Bitcoin's blockchain – but they also attain a level of reliability that no human-made agreement could ever aspire to. In a technical Yellow Paper published in 2015, Gavin Wood, a British computer scientist who – alongside Buterin and Jeffrey Wilcke, another developer – would write most of Ethereum's code, put it this way: 'The incorruptibility of judgement, often difficult to find, comes naturally from a disinterested algorithmic interpreter.'[6]

'Transparency,' he goes on to say, 'or being able to see exactly how a state or judgement came about through the transaction log and rules or instructional codes, never happens perfectly in human-based systems since natural language is necessarily vague, information is often lacking, and plain old prejudices are difficult to shake.'

There is a profoundly political backstory to that stance. Speaking in 2019, Wood recalled that, five years earlier, when former NSA contractor Edward Snowden revealed the US's global surveillance programme, Wood felt a deep affinity. 'I realised that what I was working on, Ethereum, was fundamentally part of the same overall movement,' he said. This movement, which he christened Web3,[7] aimed to replace opaque and overbearing centres of power with transparent networks. 'You can boil the Web3 mantra down to: "less trust and more truth".'

From the Ethereum point of view then, dealing with human counterparts and organisations always entails trust – trust that they say what they mean; trust that they act rationally; trust that they are not crooks; trust that they won't spy on you. The rules underpinning self-enforcing smart contracts, on the other hand, are *trustless.* They are on the blockchain for everyone to see, and they do exactly as they say, demanding no leap of faith. That, of course, assumes that perusing a smart contract's code is enough to pin down its effects. It is a dangerous assumption, and one that would come back to bite the Ethereum community.

Having computer code execute a set of instructions would not be, per se, particularly impressive. After all, that is how the internet works: ordering an e-book on your Kindle or buying a song on iTunes requires making a payment, which kick-starts a process, which culminates in the delivery of a digital product. Once again it is the architecture that is supposed to make the difference. 'Smart contracts' programs could be run anywhere,' says Karl Floersch, a core researcher at the Ethereum Foundation. 'They could be run in Google Cloud, they could be run in Amazon Web Services. But the reason why they're run in Ethereum – and the reason why it has so much weird value attached to it – is because of the guarantees that the Ethereum system provides. Those guarantees being that they're not going to go down, you can't be censored, you can't be stopped. No one can flip the kill switch for a particular application on the system.'

Once again it is the decentralisation magic, applied not only to payments, but also to whole financial operations, or to software applications (in fact, to their back end – elements such as an app's user interface are hard to build directly on the blockchain).

To do that, Ethereum has had to be designed to take into account not only monetary balances, but also changes in digital states. Every full node on the Ethereum blockchain includes a copy of the Ethereum

Virtual Machine (EVM), a digital environment where smart contracts are executed. When an Ethereum block is mined – usually in 10–20 seconds – it fixes in time the whole array of relationships and exchanges taking place on the network at a given time.

In a 2017 interview,[8] well after the launch of Ethereum, Buterin said that Bitcoin could be thought of as a software protocol tailor-made to power a currency, whereas in Ethereum 'the currency is in the service of the protocol'. For him, Ethereum was about more than Ether – it was a new tool able to spawn social networks, dropboxes, search engines, insurance companies and media conglomerates on the blockchain. It was, to cite the title of a recent book about Ethereum by journalist Camila Russo, *The Infinite Machine*. (That narrative was also one of the drivers of the blockchain fad that took hold starting from 2015 to 2016, when every business suddenly realised it needed a blockchain.)

Yet the Ether cryptocurrency is the backbone and lifeblood of the Ethereum ecosystem. Engaging with a smart contract requires the payment of Ether fees – called 'gas' – in order to both augment miners' reward and prevent vandals or attackers from clogging the network with a blizzard of small pointless transactions. One of the most popular functions of smart contracts is one that allows them to mint their own mini-currencies. And, of course, Ether itself has consistently been the second highest-priced cryptocurrency after Bitcoin.

When the Ethereum project officially kicked into gear in summer 2014, its debut was steeped in controversy over that cryptocurrency.[9] The project started with what looked like a crowdfunder: rather than letting Ether's supply build over time through mining, the Ethereum team, via Switzerland-based company Ethereum Switzerland GmbH, auctioned the bulk of the coins before its blockchain had even been built, in exchange for bitcoins.[10] Some cryptocurrency hardliners[11] looked askance at this mechanism, dubbed 'premine', because of its potential for exit scams and price manipulation, and because of its altogether less rigorous monetary foundations. As late as 2020, an old-school cypherpunk like Adam Back was railing against Ethereum on Twitter, comparing the project to a Ponzi pyramid scheme and singling out its premined structure as a scam.[12]

Clearly not every Bitcoin owner shared Back's reservations back in 2014: over 42 days, between 22 July and 2 September, Ethereum sold 60 million ethers, for the equivalent of $18 million in bitcoins.

The money raised in 2014 was funnelled into the newly created Ethereum Foundation, tasked with carrying on research into Ethereum technology. Buterin had mentioned such an organisation in his talk in Miami, saying of it, 'Eventually, we hope to turn Ethereum itself into a DAO.' The acronym stands for Decentralised Autonomous Organisation.

# Self-owning cars

Decentralised Autonomous Organisations are what you get when you combine several smart contracts – each with a different function – in order to create a business. If a smart contract is a vending machine, where you put money in and get a cup of coffee out, a DAO is the company that owns the vending machine, refills it with coffee grounds and reinvests its proceeds into new machines.

In his White Paper, Buterin defined a DAO as the 'logical extension' of smart-contract technology. DAOs were Ethereum's endgame, the main instrument to carry out its disintermediation and decentralisation agenda. Ethereum being an intrinsically economy-first world – with payments as the chief form of interaction – that decentralisation was almost inevitably focused on business. Bitcoin had been created to kill off bankers, payment companies and the Federal Reserve; among Ethereum's designated victims were CEOs. DAOs would bring about the era of manager-less corporations.

The term Decentralised Autonomous Corporation – or DAC, often used interchangeably with DAO – was coined in 2013[13] by American cryptocurrency developer Daniel Larimer. He had used it as a framework to construe cryptocurrencies at large: economic entities governed by software rules, and whose coin-owners he compared to shareholders. Vitalik Buterin took it a step forward: rather than employ them as a metaphor, why not use DAOs as a literal business model? In late 2013, in a series of articles in *Bitcoin Magazine* entitled 'Bootstrapping a Decentralized Autonomous Corporation', he laid out his theory.

'What is a corporation, after all, but a certain group of people working together under a set of specific rules?' Buterin wrote. 'However, here a very interesting question arises: do we really need the people?'

He explained that successive waves of automation had mostly undermined the blue-collar cohort – weavers, craftsmen, factory workers. Blockchain technology could do away with managers instead. His idea was simple: companies are essentially capital plus a mission statement: 'build cars', 'deliver food', 'invest in stocks'. Taking (cryptocurrency) capital as a given, Buterin's question was whether computer science could be used to 'encode the mission statement into code' and enable anyone with an idea and the coding skills to create a company out of thin air.

His answer was: probably yes. Smart contracts could be marshalled to carry out a company's vital functions, such as selling services and paying employees. Everything would exist on the blockchain, thereby removing the necessity to find a server to host the software, but also making the organisation un-takedownable, its code permanently etched on the decentralised log. That, according to Buterin, made such a model ideal for illegal businesses – which could keep operating in perpetuity without relying on any individual kingpin's survival – or for peer-to-peer online games like Buterin's old foe, *World of Warcraft*.

For Buterin, one big advantage of a DAO was its potential to solve the proverbial principal-agent problem – that is, a CEO acting against the shareholders' best interests – and in general eradicate skulduggery from the upper echelons of a business. For instance, a DAO enjoying a natural monopoly (say, a water provider) could be designed in such a way that it would be impossible for it to engage in price gouging. '[D]ecentralized corporations can be made invulnerable to corruption in ways unimaginable in human-controlled system [*sic*], although great care would certainly need to be taken not to introduce other vulnerabilities instead,' he said.

That said, Buterin was not theorising about getting rid of *all* humans. A company would still need to hire people to carry out the more creative jobs. People would be required to make hires. More importantly, someone needed to be on hand to upgrade the DAO's software, if the code were found to be faulty. Buterin proposed several solutions, one of which was pretty simple: a DAO could have human shareholders, able to vote on complex decisions without going through a board or CEO. If one were to bring it back to Daniel Larimer's analogy, those shares might actually be units of cryptocurrency. (Keep this idea in mind, as we'll meet it again.)

At the time Buterin did not suggest that DAOs should be built on Ethereum – if only because he wrote his articles before the Ethereum White Paper's publication.

But when the paper came out, a large section of it was devoted to DAOs, and it built extensively on his *Bitcoin Magazine* series.

In mainstreaming the concept of DAO, Buterin was not acting in a vacuum. The cryptocurrency scene was then increasingly warming to the idea that digital cash could go a bit further on the road to disintermediation – powering not only peer-to-peer payments between people, but payments between people and machines, people and services and even machines and machines. Mike Hearn, a British Google engineer and prominent Bitcoin developer, articulated that position in the most vivid way during a talk he gave[14] in July 2013 in Edinburgh. In his talk, Hearn introduced the idea of the self-owning car: a driverless taxi powered by Bitcoin, automatically paying for its fuel and upgrades, and belonging to no one (someone might just release it in the wild, as a public good). Over time, Hearn said, the car could even buy other cars and manage a whole fleet. Why would this be desirable? It would be absurdly cheap. That is because, Hearn went on, there would be no human intermediary 'creaming off profit' at the top. Machines would run loose, and the free market would keep prices down.[15]

What is funny about the self-owning car thought-experiment is that it is populist and anti-populist at once. It sounds like a massive middle finger flipped at Uber, Lyft and the other behemoths of platform capitalism. But it also sounds like a middle finger to every human worker.

It is sinister, but also exciting. Which is why Buterin did not let that go to waste. In Miami in 2014, although he did not mention self-owning cars, he seemed to be channelling a spirit chiming with Hearn's flight of fancy. The last word on the final slide of Buterin's presentation listed, among Ethereum's use cases, 'Skynet?': the evil artificial intelligence that takes over the world and threatens to precipitate a nuclear catastrophe in *The Terminator*. It stuck: over the following years Skynet and Ethereum were to be routinely – and a bit lazily – associated in countless media articles, promotional material and academic papers.

The Skynet reference did speak to some genuine elements of Ethereum's 'automatist' doctrine, says Jaya Klara Brekke of Durham University. 'In Ethereum, decentralisation is no longer about defying specific authorities: it is about defying any form of control by anyone whatsoever. People, human beings – let's get rid of them, since anyone is potentially corrupt.'

But Skynet was also a very catchy meme to harness, for an upstart project hoping to become the next big thing in cryptocurrency. And the DAO-as-Skynet narrative, in a bizarre way, was far too optimistic: it sounded bad for humankind, sure, but on its own terms it was a resounding success. What if a DAO were not as lucky? What if, once launched, a DAO would just malfunction, crash and burn?

# Code is law

The first DAO was called The DAO. It crashed and burned weeks after its debut, and in the process it came close to derailing the whole Ethereum project. Its short and disastrous ride began in spring 2016 – following months of announcements and media coverage – when the website daohub.org started collecting Ether in exchange for 'DAO tokens'. As previously mentioned, Ethereum allows smart contracts to mint their own mini-currencies, technically called ERC20 tokens, which can be exchanged on the platform and used for contract-specific transactions – for instance, a Ethereum-based casino might sell ERC20 poker chips to use on its platform. The DAO tokens afforded their owners the power to vote on The DAO's investment decisions.

The DAO was invented as a leaderless, employee-less, stateless venture-capital (VC) fund to invest Ether in technology start-ups. The smart-contract code underpinning it had been written and published by Christoph Jentzsch,[16] an Ethereum lead tester and co-founder of Slock.it, a Berlin-based company that aspired to blend Ethereum and Internet of Things technology (specifically, smart locks). Other co-founders included Jentzsch's brother Simon, and Stephan Tual, Ethereum's former chief communications officer. Jentzsch had originally planned to write a smart contract to crowdfund Slock.it while giving its donors a modicum of control on how the funds would be used;[17] eventually he decided to create a blueprint for something identical – almost to the letter – to Vitalik Buterin's DAO fever dream. The result was a White Paper entitled 'Decentralized autonomous organisation to automate governance'.

'Historically, corporations have only been able to act through people,' it read. 'This presents two simple and fundamental problems [...]: (1) people do not always follow the rules and (2) people do not always agree what the rules actually require.

'This paper illustrates a method that for the first time allows the creation of organizations in which (1) participants maintain direct real-time control of contributed funds and (2) governance rules are formalized, automated and enforced using software.'

The document set down the rules for building an executive-free VC firm that would automatically invest its trove of Ether in companies chosen by a majority of its token-holders – people who had contributed Ether in exchange for the organisation's ERC20 and were effectively treated as its shareholders. Any profit would be divvied up among the token-holders.

Jentzsch's blueprint was published on the code repository GitHub in early 2016. Shortly thereafter, a group of enthusiasts decided to implement it, and registered the daohub.org website to promote the project and raise the Ether that would form The DAO's venture capital. Slock.it's team was at pains to underline that the group behind The DAO's creation was independent from them, but as a matter of fact the company's co-founders became the public faces of The DAO, pitched Slock.it as a potential recipient of The DAO's investment and created a Swiss company, DAO.link, to provide The DAO (and potentially other DAOs) with legal personhood to interact with contractors. When it came to the crunch, several figures in the cryptocurrency community – as, for that matter, the US Securities and Exchange Commission –

would make out The DAO to be Slock.it's creature through and through.

The sale of The DAO tokens started on 30 April 2016 and went on until 28 May, attracting nearly 20,000 buyers. By the end of the sale The DAO's smart contract had amassed 12 million ethers – equivalent to more than $150 million, and 14 per cent of all the Ether then in circulation.[18] It was the largest crowdfunding campaign in history, and it had been used to endow a company that was run by a series of programming subroutines. By some measures, The DAO was a resounding success; by others, it was terrifying. Some thought that a multimillionaire behemoth like The DAO shouldn't have existed so early in Ethereum's history: what if something went wrong?

Sure enough, something did. On 17 June 2016 an attacker, exploiting loopholes in Ethereum's and The DAO's code, siphoned out 3.6 million ethers – about $50 million. Another separate attack followed, robbing an additional $3.5 million. Owing to a failsafe mechanism, the stolen funds would stay parked in another contract account for 28 days before the attacker could access and make away with them. Over that period, the Ethereum community engaged in two battles: one against the attacker, the other over Ethereum's soul.

One thing that tends to get lost in the business-focused mindset that The DAO epitomised is that Ethereum is not only about decentralising corporate structures and removing CEOs. A platform where contracts enforce themselves is a legal system: it also takes judges and the police out of the picture. A contract's code is the sole source of its actions, and the sole foundation of its legitimacy. Harvard scholar Primavera De Filippi and Aaron Wright, a professor at Yeshiva University, call this *lex cryptographica*.[19] In the words of lawyer and internet activist Lawrence Lessig: 'Code is Law.' Now, where did that leave The DAO's hack? Was it even a hack?

Just after the attack, Emin Gün Sirer, a professor of computer science at Cornell University who had been critical of The DAO before its launch, penned a blogpost[20] in which he said that he was chary of calling what had happened 'a hack'. If the only thing defining The DAO was its code, it was difficult to make the case that the draining of its funds ran counter to its intended purpose – as the code *did not specify* The DAO's purpose. The code had allowed for the attack to happen, hence what happened was allowed.

'There is no independent specification for what The DAO is supposed to implement,' Gün Sirer wrote. 'Heck, there are hardly any comments in The DAO code that document what the developers may have been thinking at the time they wrote the code.'

Beyond semantics – that is, even admitting that The DAO had been hacked – a more pressing question remained on what Ethereum at large should do. Developers, founders and members of the Ethereum Foundation immediately switched to war-room mode, debating on Slack and Skype – and, more publicly, on social media and blogs – how to grapple with what had happened.

Early attempts to address the catastrophe tried to ride the code to a solution. Alex Van de Sande, a designer at the Ethereum Foundation, mustered a group of volunteers under the banner of the Robin Hood Group and started hacking The DAO – exploiting its vulnerability to spirit away the remaining funds before the attacker pilfered them, too. Another early proposed fix – dubbed 'soft fork' – would have blacklisted all transactions involving the stolen funds, freezing them in place until the attacker gave them back; the scheme was later found to be flawed and was dropped. Eventually it became clear that the only way out was a 'hard fork': having miners approve an ad-hoc transaction that would erase The DAO and its hack, and return the stolen Ether to its rightful owners.

This was bound to be controversial. Yes, the snatched Ether represented a significant chunk of the network's overall supply; 10,000 users had invested in The DAO, and some key figures in the Ethereum scene – including Vitalik Buterin and, initially, Gavin Wood – had lent their credibility to The DAO as 'curators'. The incident was a tremendous reputational blow, which, if left unsolved, threatened the whole Ethereum project.

On the other hand, the reason why cryptocurrency had been invented in the first place was to ensure that no transaction – no matter how illegal – could be reversed. If you accept that code is law, then the Ethereum community's reaction to the hacking of a shoddily designed contract should have been a shrug. Especially as both Ethereum and The DAO had leaned on the Skynet narrative to the hilt: Ethereum's official website had promised 'applications that run exactly as programmed without any possibility of downtime, censorship, fraud, or third-party interference'; one of the slogans featured on daohub.org was 'The DAO is code'. And now the plan was to ignore the code and interfere?

For immutability purists – like Bitcoin core developer Peter Todd, or Nick Szabo, the inventor of smart contracts – a hard fork was a sacrilege, and a dangerous precedent. 'What is Vitalik going to say to the friendly FBI agent at the door, asking for help with a big hack on an exchange?' Todd wrote in a fuming blogpost.[21] 'Or to the Russian equivalent, who wants to freeze funds of a US exchange for trumped up reasons in retaliation against the latest round of sanctions?' Granted, there had been hard forks before: in 2010 Satoshi Nakamoto himself or herself had forced one, on realising that a bug in Bitcoin's code had created 184 billion bitcoins – well above the 21 million cap. But critics said those had been technical fixes, while Ethereum's hard fork would be the 'bailout' of an overhyped fiasco.

Three years later Vlad Zamfir,[22] a (pro-fork) Ethereum developer, would chalk up the disagreements over the hard fork to a cypherpunk shibboleth he called 'Szabo's Law'. 'Szabo's law is simple: Do not implement changes to the blockchain protocol unless the changes are required for the purpose of technical maintenance,' Zamfir wrote. Many Ethereum grandees, in contrast, were increasingly persuaded that the project would need some kind of *governance* – a dirty word among crypto-anarchists – in order to thrive.

Cornell University's Emin Gün Sirer had felt vindicated after The DAO's hack because he deemed the project to be poorly designed, but today he says the 'code is law' narrative does not hold water. 'The problem with that is that every system is human-serving. Code might be law, but if the code is not wanted, then people will change the code,' he says. 'Only code that serves the people is law. At the end of the day, there always is a governance process.'

That said, Gün Sirer thinks that during The DAO's crisis – and since – Ethereum's failure to put in place a formal governance structure has resulted in a quasi-tyranny of charismatic figures. 'If Ethereum is going to make a decision, everybody looks to Vitalik – that is the de facto centre there.'

The DAO impasse ended in July 2016: whoever owned some Ether was invited to vote – by sending a minimal amount of Ether to a certain address – on whether or not Ethereum should adopt the proposed hard fork. Only owners of about 4.5 per cent of the total Ether supply took part in the poll, but they overwhelmingly supported the hard fork. On 20 July miners approved the transaction reversing the effects of the DAO heist, and forged a new chain in the process. A minority of 'code is law' hardliners clung on to the original chain – where the DAO hack is still official history – and renamed themselves Ethereum Classic, a platform that would later become infamous for repeatedly being hacked.

As of 2020, the identity of the DAO attacker remains unknown. Stephan Tual, the Slock.it co-founder whose passionate advocacy for a hard fork had made him a lightning rod during the DAO kerfuffle, says that several clues point to the attacker being a scholar, rather than a cybercriminal. 'He was working at Swiss University with a group of researchers and that was kind of a summer project,' Tual says. Pressed for more details, Tual states that he prefers to 'let the sleeping dog lie'. He says the hacker's name is known to 'the top brasses of Ethereum'.

An unsolved whodunnit has not been the only legacy of the DAO affair, however. Its collapse has started important conversations within Ethereum about governance, the structure of Decentralised Autonomous Organisations and smart-contract security. But The

DAO ended up being more than a cautionary tale: even if the project ended in tears, it had also shown that it was possible to raise more than $150 million by selling intangible tokens on a blockchain. What was everybody waiting for?

3

# The ICO bubble

## The magic-money spree

Ethereum had begotten The DAO, and The DAO had begotten discord and the threat of disaster. But while the fever dream of the self-running business lost some of its lustre, The DAO's model of raising funds – hundreds of millions, indeed – was only getting started.

The crowdfunding of cryptocurrency projects by selling hosts of digital tokens had in fact pre-dated the 2016 heist. The first entity to do so had been Mastercoin – a Bitcoin 2.0 venture with which Vitalik Buterin had collaborated in his pre-Ethereum days, and which had raised about $500,000 from the sale of its tokens in 2013. The launch of Ethereum itself, powered by the auction of billions of premined ethers, had also been in that tradition. But things only really got going in late 2016 and throughout 2017, with The DAO's ashes still warm, as more and more tokens started to pop up, promoted by a variegate crowd eager to sell them on the market. Suddenly cryptocurrency had entered the era of the token sale or, to use a finance-redolent term popular in those months, the era of the Initial Coin Offering – the ICO.

The logic underpinning the idea of ICO is best explained with a metaphor. Imagine you want to open a supermarket. The problem is: you are broke, and nobody wants to lend you money to kick-start the business. However, you come up with a brilliant plan: what if you printed a limited number of loyalty cards, to be used in your future supermarket, and sold them to raise the capital you need? Future patrons, who like your supermarket concept and maybe live near the site you have chosen, would kill two birds with one stone if they came on board: they would help bring about the supermarket, and get some loyalty cards affording them discounts and perks once the supermarket is open. Given that you only made a finite number of those cards, buyers could theoretically scalp their exclusive loyalty cards at a higher price if the buzz around the soon-to-be-built supermarket grows. Now change 'loyalty cards' to 'cryptocurrency tokens' and 'supermarket' to 'blockchain-based company', and that's the ICO craze in a nutshell. In 2017 many people realised that cryptocurrency technology – and Ethereum in particular – enabled them to mint their loyalty cards and crowdfund their intangible supermarkets.

If the history of cryptocurrency is one of increasing disintermediation – or, at least, a history of successive *waves of rhetoric* about disintermediation – the spin put on ICOs was that they would slay a sector-specific middleman: the venture capitalist. Tokens would tear down all barriers for accessing funds for promising start-ups: anyone with an idea, especially cryptocurrency- or blockchain-related, could bypass venture capitalists and institutional investors and raise funds directly from future users, in exchange for tokens granting them some benefits once the project had been built. On the flipside, wannabe technology investors would also be empowered by the mechanism: tokens would be a way to invest in companies they liked, even if they did not have the buckets of Saudi or pension-fund cash and high-value connections VC firms can rely on. Professional investors would be replaced with a direct relationship between small-time investors – or fans – and company founders. J. R. Willett, the developer behind Mastercoin and self-styled inventor of the ICO,[1] pushed hard on that narrative during a round table on the future of Bitcoin in 2013.[2] 'If you wanted to, today, start a new protocol layer on top of Bitcoin, a lot of people don't realise, you could do it without going to a bunch of venture capitalists,' he said.

'If you get a bunch of trustworthy guys together that people have heard of and say, okay, we're going to do this: we're going to make a new protocol layer. It's going to have new features X, Y and Z on top of Bitcoin, and here's who we are and here's our plan, and here's our Bitcoin address, and anybody who sends coins to this address owns a piece of our new protocol – anybody could do that.'

It was a bit like a crowdfunding campaign on the Kickstarter platform, but decentralised – Kickstarter is a middleman after all – and with a cryptocurrency twist adding a shareholding-like feel (a donor 'owns a piece of our new protocol' – a concept bound to create headaches galore). And ICOs were touted as a solution not only to VC firms' gatekeeping, but also to the general difficulty in raising funds for open-source projects – as most blockchain protocols are.

Jamie Burke, a venture capitalist and CEO of Outlier Ventures, told me[3] in 2017 that, thanks to ICOs, 'for the first time ever, open-source initiatives can be profitable for investors'.

'Previously, [these initiatives] were relying upon donations and they were inherently unprofitable – people would just do them for an ethical goal. Now there is a financial incentive for people to participate.' The financial incentive being that – like our unfinished supermarket's loyalty cards – once the project took off, its tokens could be resold for a return on cryptocurrency exchanges or secondary markets, their value waxing or waning according to the iron law of supply and demand.

Now that narrative was exciting, and consistent with the 'stick-it-to-the-man' spirit that had shaped cryptocurrency since its early days. However, when you go from theory to practice, that perfect edifice of peer-to-peer VC economy starts to creak. Using decentralised, pseudonymous, unregulated platforms to raise funds for still-to-be-built projects is bound to attract some less than savoury individuals selling nothing in exchange for something. Moreover, at a time when everyone was marvelling at Bitcoin's and Ethereum's staggering price spikes, everyone – from Bitcoin barons to amateur traders in their living rooms – wanted to be an early investor in a token that stood a chance of becoming valuable further down the road: speculation took precedence over genuine interest in funding clever start-up ideas. Mix and shake and you end up with what a *Forbes* cover called 'the craziest bubble ever'.

# Bubbly unicorns

So it is 2017 and you want to launch an ICO. First, you will need a White Paper: a PDF explaining what company or service you wish to launch. It might include some of the code you will use to build your product, but that is not strictly necessary. What is necessary is writing something that looks official enough – but not nearly as detailed and verifiable as an Initial Public Offering's prospectus. It can even involve some degree of plagiarism[4] of past White Papers from successful ICOs, to speed things up.

The key portion of the White Paper, however, will be devoted to explaining how the token sale works. Most ICOs[5] – starting with The DAO – use Ethereum's ERC20 tokens. The tokens will be issued through a smart contract, programmed to return a certain number of tokens in exchange for a certain quantity of ethers – a fact that during the ICO frenzy made the price of Ether skyrocket,[6] as prospective investors stockpiled it to partake in ICOs. (Bitcoin also reached the then all-time-high price of $19,783.06 in December 2017, but the causes of that vertiginous rise are less immediately discernible.)

In spite of the democratising rhetoric, it is not uncommon for a project launching an ICO to sell a percentage of its tokens in a premine – a behind-closed-doors agreement in which accredited investors, ready to stump up high quantities of ethers or bitcoins, can secure baskets of tokens at a discount. But once that is over, most of the energy of the people behind an ICO will be devoted to drumming up the hype in order to lure as many people as possible into participating in the 'crowdsale' – that is, the online auction of the bulk of the tokens.

There will be pitches at technology events, slick videos hawking the ICO as the next big thing, and groups on social-media and messaging apps to rally the fans ahead of the sale. There will be a website featuring the names of team members and those of high-profile technical advisers or celebrities[7] lending their names and faces to the project. In some cases, the advisers really endorse the projects; in others, they will find out too late that their reputation has been hijacked by con artists. The website also features a countdown to the day of the crowdsale.

The auction itself can take various forms, all of which have downsides. Vitalik Buterin himself, in June 2017, as the platform he had built was creaking under the weight of the writhing blob of token-peddlers, wrote a long blogpost[8] analysing the game-theoretical nightmare that ICO auctions presented. At the time an ICO could be 'uncapped' – that is, accept all the money people are ready to throw at it, and emit tokens accordingly. Yet that risks flooding the company with way too much (crypto) cash and catching the eye of regulators: bad in general for a cryptocurrency venture, and bad in particular when you are selling quasi-financial instruments in an ill-defined legal ecosystem. Alternatively, a sale could be 'capped' in such a way that the ICO will only accept funds until it hits a given threshold ($5 million, £100,000, 1,500 ethers, etc.). The risk here is that the ICO will be over within seconds, as crazed buyers rush to hoover up all the tokens, leaving many other prospective buyers empty-handed. Indeed, such flash-sales became a fixture of the ICO Halcyon Days. In April 2017 an ICO run by blockchain-based prediction market Gnosis raised $12.5 million in 12 minutes; the next month the ICO for a token associated with a browser called Brave raised $35 million – in 30 seconds. Further complicating the matter was the fact that in most cases the company behind an ICO would keep a big lump of tokens for itself and pay its employees in tokens, engendering a myriad of bad incentives to manipulate the sale and the token's price.[9]

But despite all those complications and red flags, tokens – also known among critics as 'shitcoins' – were taking the world by storm. By the end of 2017 a report by VC firm Fabric Venture and cryptocurrency consultancy TokenData calculated that ICOs had raised $5.6 billion.[10] Some of that money went to projects that were dubious, or downright unserious: even the joke ICO Useless Ethereum Token, its logo a middle finger, raised $62,000. Fear of missing out, combined with bustling online markets and exchanges where these tokens could be traded and speculated on with no restriction or regulatory oversight, visited upon the world a full-blown cryptobubble – a scramble for digital coins supposed to be spent on still-to-be-built online platforms. In his blogpost, Buterin acknowledged the risk inherent in the offerings that were being made, with the hyper-pragmatic caveat that the bubble was not the result of buyers being gullible or irrational. 'There is certainly a weird bubbliness about crypto-assets,' he wrote. 'However, there's a strong case to be made that the participants at the sale stage are in many cases doing nothing wrong, at least for themselves.' As long as the bubble kept ballooning, stashing tokens was the rational thing to do: a 2018 study[11] by Boston College scholars Hugo Benedetti and Leonard Kostovetsky found that, on average, tokens appreciated by 179 per cent from the day of the ICO to the day they start being traded on online platforms. (Hence the safest strategy was buying tokens in an ICO and selling them as soon as they were listed online.)

The story of the biggest ICO in history vividly encapsulates those heady days. Called EOS, it proposed to build a new blockchain that would rival Ethereum in versatility and power. Its promoters, acting under the aegis of Cayman Islands-based company Block.one, were prominent figures in the cryptocurrency space. The chief developer was Daniel Larimer, the first proponent of the concept of DAO.[12] The ICO's public face was Brock Pierce, a former child actor who had starred in Disney flicks *The Mighty Ducks* and *First Kid,* before embarking on a career as a technology entrepreneur. His first venture had been Digital Entertainment Network, a proto-Netflix that imploded in 2000 when Pierce and his co-founder were accused of child sexual abuse (charges against Pierce were later dismissed, whereas the company's CEO, Marc Collins-Rector, was convicted). Straight after that, Pierce had launched Internet Gaming Entertainment (IGE), a company that employed thousands of gamers to play online games such as *World of Warcraft* for hours on end to obtain special digital objects – 'gold' – that IGE resold for dollars to gamers who could not be bothered finding their own gold. While at IGE, Pierce hired Stephen K. Bannon – the man who would later become US president Donald Trump's chief ideologue and strategist, but who back then was simply a film producer with a background in investment banking. Bannon would eventually replace Pierce as IGE's CEO in 2007, and the two remain close. After IGE, the transition from peddling in-game 'gold' to cryptocurrency and ICOs had been almost natural to Pierce, who had been among the co-founders of Willet's Mastercoin. 'My entire life I have been doing the same thing,' he told me in 2017[13] when I met him during his EOS promotion roadshow.

The EOS ICO lasted for one full year, from June 2017 to June 2018, with millions of tokens sold in daily tranches. Over that period the Block.one team – often fronted by Pierce – toured the world to huckster the project at technology conferences, meet-ups and glitzy all-night-long parties. Pierce, decked out in a futuristic cowboy attire and tinkling pendants shaped like cryptocurrency symbols, was light on details of what EOS would achieve and big on inspiring talk, forecasting a cryptocurrency-fuelled utopia modelled after Burning Man – the nudity-friendly festival popular with the Silicon Valley crowd that takes place every year in the Nevada desert. Pierce would leave Block.one in March 2018, shortly after comedian John Oliver ridiculed Pierce's Burning Man proselytising, bombastic promises and unicorn-themed wedding (which took place at Burning Man) on his late-night show. Undeterred, Pierce refocused his efforts on creating a cryptocurrency community in disaster-stricken Puerto Rico; in 2020 he ran for US president as an independent, on a pro-technology platform.

EOS's ICO ended up selling one billion ERC20 tokens for $4.2 billion in ethers, becoming the most successful token sale ever. Before the sale started, Block.one had declared it would not invest in the sale, lest it interfere with the auction and artificially pump the token's price by rerouting the ethers it received back into its own ICO. The restriction did not apply to individual Block.one members. The press reported[14] with bafflement how the tokens that had just earned Block.one a treasure were described on EOS's website as 'not hav[ing] any rights, uses, purpose, attributes, functionalities or features'. Legally speaking, they were worse than useless.

On the plus side, at least EOS's blockchain was actually built and launched (in June 2018) and today is a moderately successful initiative. That outcome was far from guaranteed in most cases. Many projects made it clear that they might eventually not deliver a product, and characterised the funds raised in their ICOs as 'donations'. The Boston University study estimated that 56 per cent of the projects that had conducted a token sale up to April 2018 had gone silent within 120 days of the ICO. A report[15] by EY (Ernst & Young) published shortly thereafter – in October 2018 – found that out of the 86 most successful ICOs conducted in 2017, only one-third had launched a product or a prototype one year later. As of August 2020, the crowdsourced website deadcoins. com[16] listed 1,928 tokens as parodies, deceased, hacked or scams. Some of these scams have become sufficiently infamous to have attained quasi-legendary status, the textbook case being OneCoin, a $4 billion Ponzi scheme whose parable would later be explored in the BBC's hit podcast *The Missing Cryptoqueen.*

There was way too much money swirling around, and some people were starting to get hurt. Despite the Wild West, devil-may-care spirit pervading many of these projects, ICOs were not happening in a dusty saloon or on another planet. They were taking place in countries with clear rules about the sale of financial products. Authorities might have scratched their heads for a while when trying to make ICOs fit in preordained categories, but they took notice, albeit ploddingly. They just couldn't ignore what was happening with ICOs any longer. And they didn't.

# Law is law

What is a token? A lot of the regulatory debate, and the regulatory realities, around ICOs hinged on answering that semantic question. A token is a string of code on Ethereum. It is a digital asset. It is a device for speculation. It is – in the direst cases – a signifier of one's gullibility.

In 2017 it was also a legal unknown, which made it legal dynamite. Bitcoin, with its anonymous founder, decentralised nature and pseudonymous features, had more or less got away with being an extra-legal construct, which could not be crushed simply because there was no single person or company to bear upon. Ethereum had charismatic, yet officially powerless, leaders like Buterin, but still enjoyed some of the impalpable nature of its predecessor. In contrast, ICOs – or at least ICOs that did not want to be immediately shrugged off as scams – needed to be explicitly chalked up to a company and a person, who would ultimately carry the can if anything untoward happened. Cryptocurrency had been spawned by a subculture that accepted no authority and no law. Now, as that technology was turned into an instrument to make a killing by selling White Paper-backed promises and digital coins, the idea that code was law was shattered by the tune of jangling handcuffs and early-morning knocks at the door. Code was not the only law to heed; depending on where one was based and the law of the land, *law was law*.

That is why, despite J. R. Willett's initial vision of doling out 'a piece of our new protocol' to each buyer, most of the start-ups running ICOs soon learned to steer clear of that model – at least ostensibly. The problem with Willett's notion was that it made ICOs sound an awful lot like selling securities. And that opened a regulatory can of worms.

In the United States an asset does not have to be explicitly labelled as a security to be regarded as one by the US Securities and Exchange Commission (SEC). Since *SEC v. W. J. Howey Co.* – a seminal 1946 Supreme Court case centred on a Florida orange grove – the SEC's definition of security has encompassed 'investment contracts', understood as transactions 'whereby a person invests his money in a common enterprise and is led to expect profits solely from the efforts of the promoter or a third party'. Any company selling tokens that meet those criteria risks being prosecuted for selling securities without having gone through the SEC's process of vetting and registration – or applying for an exemption. To hammer the point home, in the summer of 2017 – with the ICO mania at full tilt – the SEC published an 18-page report[17] about The DAO. It concluded that the abortive Skynet's ICO had indeed been an illegal securities sale orchestrated by Slock.it. No action was taken: the report was intended more as a signpost, warning companies against being cavalier with their ICO plans. Nobody could plead ignorance any more: if they had sold tokens to US citizens, they could rest assured that the SEC would be on their case.

Already before (but even more so after) the SEC's warning, several projects had tried to minimise the likelihood of landing in the regulator's crosshairs. The facile way of doing so involved stating in the White Paper that the tokens were not securities, or forbidding US citizens from participating in the ICO – and hoping they would not use technical stratagems to buy the tokens regardless. Another way was structuring one's token as a 'utility', something that has clear uses on the platform to which it is linked – chips on a blockchain-based casino, or a mini-currency that can be spent to rent file-storage space on a blockchain-based cloud-storage service. Essentially a utility token is bought to be used, not held and resold at a higher price.

The problem with that is that a company's interpretation of its token's attributes can differ from the SEC's. Take as an example Kik, a Canadian messaging app that, in 2017, raised $100 million by selling Kin tokens, whose declared function was acting as a payment system for the app's users. The promoters of Kin thought they were selling a new 'general-purpose cryptocurrency',[18] and that a currency would be almost by definition a utility token. (In October 2019 the SEC would indeed state that bitcoins are not securities, given that 'current purchasers of Bitcoin are [not] relying on the essential managerial and entrepreneurial efforts of others to produce a profit'.[19]) The SEC, though, had other ideas: in June 2019 it charged[20] Kik with making an illegal securities offering, on the ground that Kin tokens were marketed 'as an investment opportunity'. The SEC's position was that regardless of a token's functionality, the marketing around it and its distribution method were enough grounds to brand it a security. As of 2020, Kik was still jostling with the SEC over definitions, but the battle had taken a toll: in September 2019 the company announced that it would shut down its app[21] and redirect all its resources to the confrontation with the SEC. Telegram, another popular messaging app that had toyed with the idea of launching a token in a public ICO – having sold $1.7 billion worth of tokens in a SEC-registered pre-sale with accredited investors in early 2018 – scrapped the plan in May 2020 after being slapped with an SEC temporary restraining order.

The SEC's general attitude to ICOs was certainly pugnacious. In a US Senate hearing in 2018 the organisation's chairman, Jay Clayton, said tersely, 'I believe every ICO I've seen is a security.'

It could be worse. Both China and South Korea banned ICOs outright in September 2017. But it could also be a lot better. For instance, in early 2018 the financial authority of Switzerland, already home to several cryptocurrency organisations – including the Ethereum Foundation – released a tripartite classification of ICO assets as 'payment tokens', 'utility tokens' or 'asset tokens'. A Switzerland-based company planning an ICO can ask the financial authority what category its token falls into, in order to make the relevant preparations to comply with money-laundering regulations (for payment tokens) or securities laws (for asset tokens). Several other countries, from the Cayman Islands to Hong Kong and Gibraltar, also bid for a role as ICO-friendly jurisdictions.

Nevertheless, by January 2018 the ICO bubble was already mid-pop. Increasing regulatory scrutiny, the mushrooming of scams, the cash-out of ICO-raised

Ether into fiat money, and tensions over the Bitcoin Cash secession have all been proffered as possible causes of the cataclysm. What we know is that a gradual sell-off of Bitcoin, Ether and every other token made the whole sector lose 80 per cent[22] of its value by September 2018. Bitcoin's price, which had hovered just under $20,000 in December 2017, had plummeted to $5,500 in November 2018. The so-called 'crypto-winter' had started.

Some observers compared the deflating to scenarios from the near-past. 'It was so similar to the dot-com bubble,' says Marc Bernegger, a Switzerland-based investor and a board member of crypto-focused holding company Crypto Finance. 'And after they realised that it was a specific period of speculation, some people in the space completely left – which is what had happened 20 years ago after the dot-com bubble burst. They need some more time to realise that crypto-assets are here to stay. But others took the opportunity to go a little bit deeper into the whole thing and realise that ICOs are not very related to the real potential and underlying power of the crypto-asset space in general.' That narrative pops up often in the industry: the ICO splurge was silly and frothy, but it is not impossible that some honest-to-God company using cryptocurrency in a smart way might clamber out of the rubble – in the same way that Amazon and eBay survived the dot-com bubble and thrived afterwards.

ICOs themselves have not disappeared completely. Some still go on under new guises and new names, such as Security Token Offerings or STOs – namely ICOs that comply with securities laws and are green-lighted by the relevant financial authorities. Another new entry is the Initial Exchange Offering (IEO): an ICO that takes place on a cryptocurrency exchange, rather than through a smart contract or another platform. A report released by consultancy PriceWaterhouseCoopers (PwC)[23] in spring 2020 calculated that in the first ten months of 2019, 380 sales – including ICOs, STOs and IEOs – had raised $4.1 billion overall; less than the estimated $5.6 billion raised in 2017[24] and the $15 billion in 2018,[25] but far from an utter disaster.

'There is still the idea of tokens,' Bernegger says. 'But the whole "Let's do an ICO and finance some fancy project" attitude, the whole industry and the whole hype around that – they have completely disappeared.'

# 4

# Stablecoins and finance

## Hodling, hoodies and suits

The ICO bubble, with its crazed trades, scammy sales and regulatory kerfuffles, had finally burst in 2018, ushering in what trade publications and Twitter pundits dubiously christened the 'crypto-winter'. The party was over. But like a bad hangover, one of its consequences was bound to linger well beyond the pop: the financialisation of cryptocurrency. It had been a process long in the making. Bitcoin was created as a means of exchange: digital money designed to bring about a dark-market economy and censorship-resistant transactions. But as its price in dollars soared, dropped and soared again – a pizza's worth of Bitcoin morphing into a paperclip's worth, and then into a yacht's – it became clear that it was better held or dumped than spent: that it was to be treated as a financial asset, not a wad of digital notes. 'Hodl', a typo-turned-internet-meme urging people to cling on to their crypto-savings, had become a watchword on social media as the token froth engulfed the planet; it was sometimes accompanied by the incantation 'to the Moon!', indicating the desired direction of a given crypto-asset's price chart. (Jokes about buying Lamborghinis – or 'Lambos' – also abounded.)

It was not only memesters and online forum-dwellers taking notice. In 2017 the Winklevoss brothers, a.k.a. 'Winklevii' – the barrel-chested identical twins who had sued Facebook's Mark Zuckerberg over allegations of finagled intellectual property – announced that their cryptocurrency exchange, Gemini, had partnered with the Chicago Board Options Exchange to launch Bitcoin futures. That same year Michael Novogratz, a heavy-hitting financier who had locked 20 per cent of his net worth in Bitcoin and Ether, kick-started a $500 million hedge fund focused on cryptocurrencies and ICOs. He exulted in a *Bloomberg* interview that the world was going through 'the largest bubble of our lifetimes'[1] and there were riches to reap.

Granted, for every Novogratz buying into the hodl mantra, there was a JPMorgan CEO Jamie Dimon calling Bitcoin 'a fraud'. (Spoiler alert: Dimon would partially eat his words just a couple of years later.) But the acceptance of cryptocurrency among more conventional investors was undeniably growing. The cryptocurrency industry, originally the preserve of hoodie-wearing coders and galaxy-brained technologists, was now dotted with sleek suits, a trend that consolidated after the ICO noise subsided. 'Three years ago, it was mainly people who were lucky to invest in Ethereum, that had a crazy performance, and they thought they were smart, because they had a few thousand per cents of luck in their performance sheets,' said Crypto Finance's Marc Bernegger in summer 2020. 'Now, most of the investors in the space are former hedge fund guys, or former professionals working at the big names on Wall Street and other financial centres.

'It's a completely different set-up also legal-wise: there's properly structured onboarding, you're not allowed to invest via cryptocurrency – you do it via traditional, fiat currency – and the whole KYC [know-your-customer regulation] applies.'

Today some of these investors are finance professionals looking for a hedge – especially, Bernegger says, 'in these uncertain times' marred by the novel coronavirus pandemic. (Whether that intuition is right is debatable: during the worst of the early stages of the coronavirus crisis, Bitcoin's price fell in unison with those of more traditional assets – essentially trailing the S&P 500; on the other hand, by January 2021, Bitcoin had zoomed to an all-time high of $41,000, with the *Financial Times* branding it an 'institutional' asset class.)

Others are family offices, organisations managing large dynastic patrimonies, keen to get a piece of this new asset class, but also more subtly fascinated by some of crypto's – especially Bitcoin's – features. 'These very traditional families have sometimes preserved their wealth for generations – and some of them experienced hyperinflation between the World Wars,' Bernegger says. 'What is alluring for them is this perspective of having new, uncorrelated, non-government-controlled assets which is somehow out of the existing system. We talk of gold 2.0.'

This trend is, however, still in its infancy, says Fiorenzo Manganiello, an adjunct professor of blockchain technologies at Geneva Business School. 'Institutional players are starting to enter the industry, but we are not talking of large numbers yet. The reason being: in order to institutionalise cryptocurrency, you'll need infrastructure. A private user can just use an online wallet, but if a bank wants to make an investment, it needs something more structured, more secure: physical wallets, or cold-storage [hardware with no internet connection to store cryptocurrency] solutions.' That is why, Manganiello says, it is noteworthy that a big chunk of investments in cryptocurrency technology in the first quarter of 2020 went into infrastructure – cold storage, cryptocurrency banking services, cryptocurrency mining.

Yet cryptocurrency finance is not the exclusive domain of suits, either. As hedge-fund managers, bankers and wealthy high-flyers woke up to the opportunities of cryptocurrency, the loose online community that had been following every twist and turn of the technology – which had been designing and testing, hodling and dumping, sneering or aiming for the Moon – also turned to finance in the wake of the ICO fever. Ethereum became the platform of choice to experiment with financial smart contracts and unleash blockchain-based entities designed for trading, lending and speculating in a more structured and coherent way than just pumping and dumping ICO tokens and hoping that no one would scam you. Slowly but steadily, a new constellation in the cryptocurrency galaxy emerged: Decentralised Finance – or DeFi.

'DeFi arose out of the ICO boom: it had created huge amounts of value kind of out of thin air, everyone was looking at this system as a big money pot,' says Ethereum Foundation's Karl Floersch. 'The question then was, "Okay, what do we actually do with this value? And how do we actually structure these systems?"

'That woke up the animal spirits in a lot of retail investors. They realised: "I now have this asset – let me trade it, let me speculate on it, let me create synthetic derivatives with it,"' Floersch continues. 'And Ethereum, because of its composability, offered a good opportunity to produce financial assets and financial instruments that interacted with one another.'

That was how DeFi finally barged in on the scene. But that is not necessarily how it started. The origins of DeFi – or at least the origins of one of the most crucial pieces in the DeFi jigsaw – actually date back to the early days of Ethereum, and even earlier than that. To understand what keeps DeFi rolling, one needs to take a step back... and talk of stablecoins.

# Looking for stability

If Bitcoin had wound up becoming an asset, that was chiefly because an awful lot of people had been persuaded that it could not be used as a currency. The reasons for that were multiple – the network was too slow and hard to scale, acceptance was patchy, it still had a whiff of illegality about it – but they mostly boiled down to volatility. No one wanted to spend bitcoins to buy apples and regret their decision after the cryptocurrency's price in dollars rocketed into the stratosphere. On the flipside, only the most radical Hayekian greengrocer would sell their apples for a digital sum whose value might have plunged by teatime. Still, unbridled speculation on exchanges, online-generated hype and panic and the absence of financial regulation made that volatility seem inevitable.

It was against this background that the concept of stablecoin emerged in the early 2010s. While stablecoins would take many forms and technical make-ups, at their core they are cryptocurrencies designed to minimise their volatility with respect to fiat currencies – typically the US dollar – or to assets such as gold or crude oil. The best way to avoid wide fluctuations in value is by relying on a reserve: keeping a unit of fiat currency (e.g. a dollar) for each unit of cryptocurrency minted, and guaranteeing that the latter can be exchanged for the former at any time.

This was, officially, the model of Tether, one of the first stablecoins ever and certainly one of the most successful. Among those launching it, in 2014, was none other than Brock Pierce – of past Mastercoin fame, and future EOS fame. (Pierce would later say he cut all ties with Tether in 2015.) Initially, Tether worked on top of the Bitcoin protocol – as a coloured coin – but over time it became tradable also on Ethereum, EOS and other blockchains.

Tether's functioning, as detailed in its White Paper,[2] is simple: a customer pays a certain amount of fiat currency to the company Tether Limited (or its sister company, Tether International Limited), in exchange for an equivalent amount of tokens – or 'tethers'. In other words, if you pay Tether $100,000, you will receive 100,000 tethers. Those tethers can be traded for other cryptocurrencies or transferred to other users, and they can be returned to Tether in exchange for the original sum of fiat cash, minus fees that constitute Tether's revenue. Once tethers have been redeemed, Tether Limited will 'burn' them – essentially make the tokens invalid – in order to maintain the fiat currency-tether tokens balance. As of September 2020, Tether Limited had created stablecoins pegged to the US dollar, the euro and the offshore Chinese yuan, and had just launched Tether Gold, a token backed by 'one troy fine ounce of gold on a London Good Delivery bar'.

From the very start, doubts were cast on Tether's claim to possess enough reserves to back up every single one of its tokens – an uncertainty that on occasion caused the tokens to be traded below the one-dollar peg, once as low as $0.92 per unit. The company, a British Virgin Islands-registered, Taiwan-based holding, kept promising an independent audit of its bank deposits, which repeatedly failed to materialise. The optics got worse in November 2017, when Tether announced[3] that an attacker had pilfered more than $30 million in tethers from the company's own wallet. One immediate effect of the hack was that Tether suspended the redemption of tokens for fiat currency: users could either keep their tethers or try to redeem them through select cryptocurrency exchanges providing such a service. When Tether finally reinstated the convertibility, in November 2018, it did so while imposing a minimum threshold of $100,000 for exchanging tethers for fiat currency – and hefty new fees. Converting tethers into dollars had gone from impossible to arduous.

What happened in the headiest months of the cryptocurrency bubble would attract more concerned scrutiny. The worry hinged on the relationship between Tether and Bitfinex, one of the world's largest cryptocurrency exchanges. Court records, and some of the documents disclosed in the Paradise Papers leak about offshore investments,[4] revealed that the two companies shared key shareholders and managers, raising questions about conflict of interest. Then in June 2018 – with Bitcoin's price fluttering around $6,000 – researchers at the University of Texas at Austin published a paper[5] that raised a much bigger red flag. The study explored whether the then-deflating Bitcoin bubble of 2017–18 had been partly the result of market manipulation orchestrated jointly by Tether and Bitfinex. By analysing the flows of Tether throughout the craze – between March 2017 and March 2018 – the researchers found that most Tether trade originated from Bitfinex, from which huge quantities of the stablecoins were moved to other exchanges and swapped for Bitcoin, boosting its price. The timing of these trades caught the researchers' attention: 'purchases with Tether are timed following market downturns and result in sizable increases in Bitcoin prices,' the paper read.

Interestingly, the tethers were firehosed out of a single entity at Bitfinex. The researchers thought this indicated either that an outsized player had invested bucketloads of dollars on Bitfinex in exchange for Tether and then immediately traded it with Bitcoin at regular intervals – or that Tether was flooding Bitfinex with stablecoins that were not backed by dollars, minting tethers out of thin air just to pump up Bitcoin's price. That, the study alleged, might be down to sheer greed: the people behind Tether might hold bitcoins whose value they wanted to maximise for personal gain, or to goose Tether's own reserves. Whatever the reason, the study strongly hinted that large quantities of tethers were being churned out, regardless of dollar parity.

Some have disputed the study's findings: apart from Tether and Bitfinex themselves, cryptocurrency consultancy LongHash argued[6] that the overall supply of tethers circulating during the bubble would have not been sufficient to effectively manipulate the market. Others have seized upon it with gusto: a consolidated class action lawsuit filed in New York in March 2020 accusing Tether and Bitfinex of market manipulation explicitly cites the paper as evidence.[7]

That was not the end of Tether's troubles. In July 2020 a New York appeals court green-lighted[8] an investigation aimed at probing, among other things, whether Tether's stablecoins were pegged to real-world dollars – a question that has grown more intriguing since late 2019, when Tether tweaked its terms of service to say that its reserves do not only include currency, but also 'cash equivalents' and other assets. By September 2020 there were more than 14 billion dollar-denominated tethers in circulation; a complete audit was still elusive, after the company admitted that only 74 per cent of its tokens were fully collateralised.

In a preternaturally fractious industry, Tether is a preternaturally beleaguered cryptocurrency. It is also one of the most important ones. In 2019 data[9] from cryptocurrency price-tracking website CoinMarketCap. com showed that Tether had overtaken Bitcoin as the most-traded cryptocurrency in the world – its monthly trading volume being on average 18 per cent higher than Bitcoin's.

The reasons for that are multifold. An August 2020 report[10] by blockchain-analysis firm Chainalysis found that, in East Asia, Tether had become the stablecoin of choice for international remittances or even full-blown capital flight. Especially in China, where the government outlawed the exchange of yuan for cryptocurrencies in 2017, Tether – which can be bought on the q.t. from brokers – is often used as the gateway for buying other cryptocurrencies. And although Tether (like the way more volatile Bitcoin before it) has not yet succeeded in becoming a widely used medium of exchange, Chainalysis found that some people in China have indeed started using it for everyday transactions.

In general, however, Tether's main-use case is as a hedge in cryptocurrency trading. 'You want a stablecoin because the asset you start with – like Bitcoin or Ether– is volatile relative to, say, the dollar,' explains Andrew Miller, the University of Illinois researcher. 'And stablecoins give you price exposure to the dollar, which is thought to be more stable.' People speculating on cryptocurrency exchanges can swap their bitcoins for tethers when they desire to lock their gains far away from the markets' fickleness. Rather than exchanging cryptocurrency for fiat currency – an operation that can take time, is taxable in certain jurisdictions and, on some exchanges, requires undergoing identity checks – they can convert it to Tether, which for all its shortcomings is widely treated as a fiat currency substitute.[11] When they want to start trading again, they can easily switch back from Tether to Bitcoin and rejoin the fray.

As a first mover, Tether has guzzled up nearly all of the stablecoin market's cake. As of July 2019, an analysis by the European Central Bank found that Tether made up 95 per cent of the global trading volume of the stablecoin market. That is not to say it is the only stablecoin in town: American cryptocurrency exchanges Coinbase and Winklevii-owned Gemini have both launched their own stablecoins. To everyone's hilarity, even JPMorgan has announced a dollar-backed JPM Coin to run on a private blockchain, with the aim of streamlining inter-bank payments.

Even if doubts remain about stablecoins' legal status and financial soundness, the market for them is booming, and investment has been flowing in by the cartload. Still, if you have been paying attention, you might have realised that stablecoins like Tether militate against everything Satoshi Nakamoto tried to accomplish when he or she launched the first cryptocurrency back in 2008. Bitcoin was conceived as open-source and transparent; Tether has never been properly audited and is dogged by unanswered questions about its reserves. Bitcoin had been hailed as a tool for removing financial middlemen; Tether *is* a middleman, and one that can blacklist users, if asked by regulators. Bitcoin's totem was decentralisation; Tether is an unabashedly centralised company, whose conduct and legal vagaries have the unique power to uphold or shatter the value of the tokens it mints.

But what alternatives might there be?

# DeFiance

One inescapable problem about creating stablecoins is the fact that dollars are not tokens. If, like Tether, a stablecoin is collateralised with fiat currencies or commodities, then that heap of cash or trove of gold bullion will have to be kept somewhere. It may be a Bahamas bank account, it may be a subterranean vault in the Alps – the route announced by the (apparently defunct) Swiss franc-backed stablecoin Rockz[12] – but someone is going to be in charge of that account, or carry the key to that vault. Those collaterals cannot be uploaded to a blockchain. If a coin is linked to real-world assets, a certain degree of centralisation will occur.

If one – true to the cypherpunk creed – wanted to reclaim decentralisation, the easiest way might be just to do away with collaterals. In 2014 British blockchain entrepreneur Robert Sams published a paper[13] suggesting that, in order to achieve stability, cryptocurrency – a technology, let us not forget, born out of spite for the Federal Reserve – should simply learn to love central banking. That did not mean embracing central *banks*: Sams still believed that centralisation, intermediation and fiat currency were ills rather than goods. But cryptocurrencies like Bitcoin, whose supply was mathematically predetermined by mining routines, were bound to see their prices savagely sway in response to rises and slumps in demand – and that was a fatal flaw for an aspiring technology whose name included 'currency'. Hence Sams's proposal: cryptocurrencies should operate in pairs – with one coin used as cash and the other used as a share. Every time demand for cash increases, the blockchain's protocol should automatically mint cash and sell it in exchange for shares, which are then immediately burned. Vice versa, when demand goes down, the protocol should issue shares and auction them for cash tokens, which are then destroyed. By tweaking the cash distribution elastically, Sams said, the cash's price would remain stable over time relative to the fiat currency of reference. 'In a sense, this dual model of coins and shares embodies the functionality of a fiat money central bank without the centralisation … or the bank,' the paper read. Code and smart contracts would take care of monetary policy.

Sams's idea (technically called the 'seigniorage shares' model, or algorithmic stablecoin) is low-cost, technically fascinating and the purest incarnation of what the Ethereum crowd today calls 'cryptoeconomics' – an informal field of research investigating how to design cryptocurrency environments by incentivising users to maintain the network rather than game it. But the algorithmic stablecoin model is a high-wire act: it requires demand for the tokens to keep growing, otherwise the auctions will flop and ruinous crashes will ensue; the cryptoeconomic gambit is just too bold. Possibly for that reason, algorithmic stablecoins have not taken off in any relevant way: some projects ended up crashing and never recovered; others were stopped in their tracks due to regulatory headaches. According to a 2019 analysis[14] by the London School of Economics and the analytics firm Blockchain.com, only 19 per cent of existing stablecoins are algorithmic – and some of those are partly backed by collaterals.

Some elements of Sams's proposal, however, survive in a more popular type of decentralised stablecoin: the cryptocurrency-collateralised stablecoin. These stable-coins' value is propped up by cryptocurrency collaterals, rather than fiat money. Given that cryptocurrency's volatility is the chief reason why stablecoins are needed in the first place, this might sound counterintuitive. The solution for that is over-collateralising the stablecoins – backing up their value with a lot of extra cryptocurrency in order to sustain the peg with the fiat currency of choice, even in the case of wild fluctuations. That is the approach taken by what is arguably the most successful decentralised stablecoin in existence – Maker DAO.

Maker DAO was one of the first projects launched on Ethereum, back in 2014. In 2016 it went close to being hit by the same disaster that doomed The DAO, with which it shared a crucial vulnerability. Luckily, the Maker team discovered the bug early on, removed the Ether from its smart contract, and the initiative remained unscathed while The DAO crumbled. In December of the following year, Maker launched its ERC20 stablecoin – Dai.

Dai is flexibly pegged to the dollar, but it is backed by Ether and a handful of other approved cryptocurrency collaterals. It is issued when users send their collaterals to Maker DAO smart contracts called Vaults, with a minimum collateral-to-Dai ratio of 150 per cent. In other words, to take out 100 Dai, a user needs to deposit the equivalent in Ether of at least $150 – as of September 2020, that is about 0.4 Ether. The collateral can be redeemed by paying back the Dai, plus a fee. (Of course, as with every other token, users can also just buy Dai on cryptocurrency exchanges.)

Most users put down a higher collateral to stave off the risk of automated liquidation. Maker DAO constantly monitors the prices of the cryptocurrencies it accepts as collateral, to ensure that every Vault's collateral is worth one and a half times the Dai it issued. If the price of a collateral – say, Ether – drops, Vaults that become under-collateralised are automatically liquidated: the Ether is auctioned for Dai, until the value of the Dai backed up by the Vault is recovered. The Dai received that way is burned – so that the balance between collateral and Dai is preserved.

Propping up the system's stability is another token – similar in some regards to the share-coin floated by Sams. Called MKR, it is a construct of cryptoeconomic incentives designed to encourage its holders to work for Maker DAO's smooth functioning, rather than engage in speculation or malicious manipulation. MKR is first and foremost a 'governance token'. Like shareholders, people owning it can vote on how to govern the ecosystem: for instance, establishing which cryptocurrencies should be accepted as collaterals or deciding to wind up the whole Maker DAO, in case of a The DAOesque attack, need for an update, or market disasters.

Focusing the voters' minds is the fact that the more Dai is minted, the more the value of MKR tokens increases: that is because when redeeming their collaterals, users need to pay a fee in MKR – which is then burned, boosting the price of the remaining tokens. By contrast, if the price of collaterals on Maker DAO crashes so dramatically that the outstanding Dai cannot be recovered via auction, the system will try to claw back funds by minting and selling new MKR – diluting the value of existing tokens and delivering a slapdown to unwise governance decisions.

Maker DAO's astutely designed architecture quickly made it the most successful cryptocurrency-backed stablecoin. In 2018 it was the first cryptocurrency initiative to attract investment from Silicon Valley VC firm Andreessen Horowitz, whose crypto-fund bought $15 million in MKR. By summer 2020 the value of the collaterals locked on its platform had passed $1 billion.

Like Tether before it, the Dai stablecoin is not widely used as currency, but as a means of creating leverage. At the most basic level, users deposit their Ether (or other collaterals) in Vaults to generate Dai, and then use the

Dai to buy more Ether, with which to generate more Dai, with which... and so on. If Ether's price collapses, that is an automated liquidation; if it goes up, users can buy the necessary Dai for Ether at a fraction of their initial cost, redeem their collaterals and cash in a net Ether gain. Of course that is a very unimaginative way of playing this game: Dai's ease of generation, its relative stability and its presence on Ethereum network, where new automated routines can be spun with a few strokes of the command line, mean that Maker DAO's token can be used as the backbone of a whole financial ecosystem.

Which brings us back to DeFi. In the aftermath of the ICO crash, Ethereum started crawling with a host of smart contracts and services – DAPPs, or decentralised applications – offering a wide range of financial operations, from loans, to futures, to exchanges, to algorithmic trading. The selling point, as usual, was disintermediation: unshackling oneself from real-world financial intermediaries, but also from cryptocurrency-focused institutions that had evolved into gatekeepers –

from Tether, to corporate cryptocurrency exchanges like Bitfinex and Coinbase. Ethereum's financial apps allowed you to trade without undergoing the identity checks, anti-money-laundering regulation and other limitations of centralised alternatives. Plus, it was much more fun.

'The advantages that DeFi has are multifold. Number one: it is in theory up 100 per cent of the time, right? So because Ethereum is always up, so is DeFi,' says Lex Sokolin, the co-head of financial technology and DeFi at blockchain software firm Consensys. 'And then there is composability, the ability to layer.'

That means that different DAPPs and smart contracts can be programmed to work in sequence, one after another, in a single transaction – their individual operations arrayed and stacked together like Lego blocks. One could easily design a program that would automatically borrow cryptocurrency from a lending platform, dump it on a decentralised exchange in the hope of making its price plummet, buy it back and return it, possibly pocketing a short margin – in a matter of seconds. Investing strategies become puzzles, jigsaws of software commands to compose on the fly.

'You can build the portfolio and when you have the portfolio, you can build margin, and when you have margin, you can build interest, and when you have interest, you can build an aggregator of fixed income, and then tokens and so on, and so forth,' Sokolin says. 'This accelerates everything, and makes it go really, really fast – I think fifty to one hundred times faster than if it were not built on DeFi.'

That sounds exciting, but it is not necessarily complication-free. 'People are building really interesting – but mostly experimental – tools. These are being built mostly by amateurs who do not understand how actual finance works,' says Emin Gün Sirer, the Cornell professor. 'So some of these "Lego building blocks" are quite interesting and do things that Wall Street cannot do. But some of them end up interacting in unforeseen ways.'

Exhibit A: the infamous 'flash loan' incident that sent waves through cryptoland on St Valentine's Day 2020. On that day an anonymous trader managed to get away with a profit of $350,000 in Ether from lending platform bZx, after deliberately pumping asset prices on the exchange bZx relied upon to get its pricing data. The best bit? The money used in the *coup de main* had been borrowed from a platform that allowed users to take cryptocurrency loans – for a very short period of time: hence 'flash loan' – without providing collateral. The trader had transformed no money into a lot of money. Cue a debate redolent of the DAO hack, regarding whether the trader could be labelled 'a hacker' or simply someone who had read the fine print, realised that bZx could be gamed and acted accordingly.

Glimpses of future headaches are already peeking over the horizon. As of autumn 2020, the hottest DeFi development was 'yield farming', a mechanism to earn new cryptocurrency tokens just by depositing other tokens on decentralised lending markets. DAOs, intended once again as manager-less, token-governed platforms, were making a self-assured comeback. ICOs were no more, but the scramble to grab the governance tokens *du jour*, and get a piece of this or that DeFi protocol, was deeply redolent of 2017 – even if research suggests[15] that the people engaging in this new gold rush are more financially literate than the poor saps who lost their shirts in the ICO frenzy.

As of August 2020, about $5 billion in Ether and Bitcoin was underpinning DeFi protocols – far from an eye-watering sum, but growing quickly. In December 2019 that figure was closer to $1 billion in cryptocurrencies. Where this leads is anybody's guess. Karl Floersch, the Ethereum Foundation researcher, thinks there is risk that a 'cascading failure' could simply put an end to it all. 'Let's say that Maker DAO becomes massively under-collateralised:[16] they mint a bunch of MKR but it's not enough. And all of the systems that rely on it go down – and everything goes down all together,' he says. 'There are kind of crazier risks like regulation, massive internet censorship, but I don't think that those are quite as poignant as just a simple market failure. These projects are new, experimental, crazy. The people who build them are, honestly, real risk-takers.'

Jamie Burke, the UK-based CEO of Outlier Ventures, believes that for all its buccaneering experimentation, DeFi will eventually mature and be co-opted back into mainstream finance. 'I think of DeFi as a sandbox: I've got a concept. I can test, validate that concept. I can understand the economics of it in this permissionless sandbox that is DeFi. Once I have done that, I can then raise money, I can hire the lawyers,' he says. 'Ultimately, if you want mainstream users, the reality is that the average person wants the insurance policy of a regulated product.

'ICOs are a really good example: everybody is all for ICOs and low levels of regulatory burden as long as they're making money. The minute that they're losing money, guess what? They become claimants for class-action lawsuits. So the idea that DeFi is somehow going to create a parallel system is nonsense.'

For the time being, the most lasting consequence of the DeFi boom is that it took Ethereum by storm.

The 'infinite machine' is now more like an online zany Wall Street on LSD. That is prompting the project's developing team to grapple with questions of scalability and speed – questions that were on the cards from the get-go, but have now acquired a new urgency. As of 2020, the project was warming up for a staggered transition to a new architecture known as Ethereum 2.0 or Eth2. One big change will be the end of proof-of-work in favour of proof-of-stake – a process in which nodes verify transactions not by burning electricity through mining, but by down-paying a certain amount of Ether, which will be lost if they wave through an invalid transaction. The restructuring, which includes other major changes alongside proof-of-stake, aims at eventually bringing Ethereum's capacity to 100,000 transactions per second – up from the current 15.

Vitalik Buterin himself outlined the various steps of the long journey to Eth2 in a series of detailed blogposts published in October 2019. But not everyone was listening. In those months, governments and regulators worldwide were indeed fretting about cryptocurrencies and the risk they posed to financial stability – but they were not worried that those threats would come from Ethereum or, for that matter, from Bitcoin, or Tether, or Dai. They were looking elsewhere: to Silicon Valley.

# 5
# Libra

## Facecoin

Stablecoins have become the lynchpin of cryptocurrency finance, playing the role of safe havens to park one's profits between bouts of speculation. Tether is gaining traction as a medium of exchange in some parts of Asia but, for the most part, stablecoins are used as hedges, not currencies. As a whole, cryptocurrencies are still too technically limited, too tainted with memories of crimes and scandals and – crucially – too niche to be seen as serious competitors for mainstream payment systems. While the overall number of blockchain-based wallets has jumped from 10 million in 2016 to 50 million in 2020[1] (that does not mean 50 million people are using cryptocurrency: one user often juggles several wallets), that is a far cry from the 1.1 billion Visa or the 939 million Mastercard credit cards in circulation as of 2020. While they are increasing, cryptocurrencies' rates of adoption and acceptance are just too low for it to work as proper money.

What would it take to change that? The solution would appear to be a cryptocurrency that can rely on a formidable technical infrastructure to solve scalability and delay issues; that is associated with an organisation that is already so well known there can be no question about the cryptocurrency's legitimacy; and one that can be distributed to a huge and established group of users, piggybacking the network effect to mass adoption. Who on Earth might be able to pull that off?

Facebook, Inc., the US social-network behemoth comprising Facebook, Instagram and WhatsApp, announced the launch of its blockchain research unit in May 2018. Heading it would be David Marcus, previously in charge of Facebook Messenger and a veteran of the payment sector, who had once led PayPal and still sat on the board of cryptocurrency exchange Coinbase. Marcus was a star employee, not one to keep busy on an otiose experiment: Facebook was serious about doing something with blockchain tech. That was confirmed in February 2019 when Facebook acquired UK start-up Chainspace, whose research team, led by George Danezis – an information security academic at University College London – had been working on how to build scalable, fast and secure blockchains.

Whatever Facebook was up to, it was doing it in the midst of the most serious PR crisis it had ever confronted. In early 2018 a series of articles in Britain's *Observer* and in the *New York Times* revealed that the social network had allowed the political consultancy Cambridge Analytica to harvest the data of up to 87 million users, potentially to build psychological profiles and target some of them with bespoke ads on behalf of Donald Trump's presidential campaign in 2016. More scandals piled on – from accusations that Facebook was not doing enough to stem the spread of 'fake news' and disinformation being posted on the site, to the revelation that it had hired an opposition research firm to smear its critics. When Mark Zuckerberg was being grilled before the US Senate for ten hours on topics ranging from Russian interference to genocidal violence in Myanmar, one would have been forgiven for not paying too much attention to the company's blockchain manoeuvres.

News of Facebook's novel venture emerged on 18 June 2019, when a video was posted on the site showing soppy footage of people in Asian cities selling their merchandise and counting wads of banknotes. A voiceover announced the advent of something called Libra. 'Join us as we move towards a world where money works for everyone,' the voice said. At long last Facebook was stepping into the cryptocurrency arena. There was a Libra website and several social-media accounts. There was a White Paper, and reams of detailed technical documents – many of them signed by Danezis and other Chainspace alums – detailing how Libra would help bring about financial inclusion of the 1.7 billion people across the globe who lacked access to banks or financial services. The scale of Facebook's ambition was immediately evident, and staggering. Slated to launch in 2020, Libra was intended to be nothing less than a private global currency.

Libra was designed as a stablecoin which, to avoid dramatic changes in value over time, was pegged not to one particular legal tender like the dollar or the euro, but to a 'basket' of different currencies and low-risk assets, such as bank deposits and government securities. This meant that while Libra's price vis-à-vis a specific currency could fluctuate, its value would not change dramatically over time. People would buy Libra for cash from authorised sellers, then transfer it to other people – paying trifling fees – or use it to buy stuff online or offline from merchants that accepted it. The cash would be added to Libra's reserve, guaranteeing that every Libra coin could be redeemed for cash.

Facebook was the motor of the whole enterprise, but the company was at pains to clarify that it would not be running Libra alone. Rather, overall control would be in the hands of the Libra Association, a Geneva-based non-profit organisation, whose members included tech and finance big cheeses such as Uber, Lyft, Spotify, Andreessen Horowitz, Coinbase, PayPal, Stripe, Visa, Mastercard and eBay, among others. Each of the 28 members would pony up $10 million to endow Libra with capital, take a cut of the profits from transfer fees and interest on the reserve's financial assets, and run one of the nodes of the Libra network. While the blockchain was 'permissioned' – only the 28 members could run nodes, as opposed to anyone with the servers and the power – it aimed to move to an open-source, 'permissionless' make-up within five years.

Fun facts about the Libra blockchain: it did not feature proof-of-work mining, or proof-of-stake; it did not feature blocks. That made many wonder whether it could be called a blockchain at all or, for that matter, whether Libra should be called a cryptocurrency. Was this all just a PR-savvy bit of branding?

Perhaps. But Facebook's game was crystal-clear. The social-networking giant was officially part of the Libra Association under the guise of Calibra, a subsidiary led by Marcus, but Facebook had been the cryptocurrency's architect and Libra was unquestionably Facebook's brainchild. Calibra had designed a Libra wallet to be integrated with WhatsApp and Messenger, allowing users to send each other cash via text. That would, theoretically, fulfil Libra's 'bank the unbanked' vision: every person living in a financially under-served area could pay, and be paid, through Calibra on their phone, send remittances quickly and with low tariffs, and use financial services that Libra would make accessible. But while the downtrodden were bandied about – front and centre – in Libra's PR material, Libra's potential user base could end up being much larger, including anyone with an account on Facebook, WhatsApp or Instagram – that is, about 2.7 billion people. Now *that* is something a global (crypto)currency could work with. The question was: will they let it?

# Libra libre

A company that was still reeling from a string of scandals about privacy and data protection was never going to be given an easy ride when spearheading an effort to create a global currency. By 2019 few people trusted Facebook with their data; who would trust it with their money?

Questions immediately arose about whether the Calibra wallet payment history would be connected to Facebook profiles, to tailor and target ads based on users' financial operations. Such a pairing lent itself to unsavoury scenarios, from e-commerce websites tweaking their prices depending on one's Libra balance, to the targeting of payday-loan ads to financially struggling users. Facebook immediately clarified that Libra's financial data 'will not be used to improve ad targeting on [...] Facebook', but the company's chequered history with promises kept the privacy advocates doubting. Plus, there were caveats: Calibra data might be shared with

Facebook in case that was needed to comply with the law, or when the users had given their consent.

A line in the White Paper raised more eyebrows: 'An additional goal of the association is to develop and promote an open identity standard.' It read like a throwaway remark, shrouded in the customary reassurances about privacy and decentralisation, but to some people it sounded as though Facebook and its chums were trying to build a digital ID system.

The cryptocurrency community was predictably sceptical. Just over a decade earlier Satoshi Nakamoto had laid down the urtext of cryptocurrency, with the goal of cutting out middlemen, scattering centres of power on an online ledger and creating a pseudonymous payment system that could not be hijacked or censored. Now Facebook – a technology monopoly in the business of monetising people's identities – might be on the verge of disintermediating money, simply by replacing the world's banking system with a members-only club of megacorporations. Vitalik Buterin's comment, in a media interview, was curt: Libra was simply 'not the best for privacy'. A few days after Libra's unveiling, Mustafa Al-Bassam, the only Chainspace co-founder who had refused to join Facebook in 2019 – and a former leader of hacking outfit LulzSec – let rip in a long Twitter thread[2] lambasting Libra's lack of decentralisation. 'My concern is that Libra could end up creating a financial system that is \*less\* censorship-resistant than our current traditional financial system,' he wrote. After all, Al-Bassam said, the world is dotted with thousands of banks in different countries, which theoretically allows for independent action on an individual bank's part. Libra would be run by a closed network of 28 blue-chip companies amenable to the Swiss courts – which might in some cases require them to block or reverse transactions.

Others were worried about the repercussions Libra might have for the cryptocurrency industry at large. Consensys's Lex Sokolin, speaking in summer 2020 – when the Libra roadmap had already undergone an emasculating overhaul – thought the project's sheer size might drain users and talent away from open-source environments like Ethereum. 'If commerce isn't happening on the Ethereum network – you're going to lose developers, you're going to lose asset movements. You're going to lose,' he says. 'It's gonna be a desert. These networks are winner-takes-all.'

But the people fretting most about Libra were not technologists or cypherpunks. They were governments.

Shortly after the Libra announcement, French finance minister Bruno Le Maire thundered against Facebook's plans to create 'a sovereign currency' and made it clear that he would stand in the way of what he perceived to be a threat to nation states' political and monetary sovereignty. He swiftly started rallying forces within the eurozone to oppose the project's launch in Europe. China, a country where mobile payments via apps like WeChat Pay or AliPay were already ubiquitous, regarded Libra with extreme mistrust. 'If the digital currency is closely associated with the US dollar, it could create a scenario under which sovereign currencies would coexist with

US dollar-centric digital currencies,' Wang Xin, director of the People's Bank of China's research bureau, said at a conference in July 2019.[3] 'There would be in essence one boss, that is the US dollar and the United States.'

Ironically, American politicians across the political spectrum did not seem to see Libra's potential as an instrument of US soft power. Maxine Waters, the Democratic chair of the House Committee on Financial Services, asked Facebook to put the project on ice on the very day Libra was announced. A few weeks later President Donald Trump took to Twitter[4] to air his concerns about the plan – accusing cryptocurrencies of being a conduit for dirty money, and stating that 'Facebook Libra's "virtual currency" will have little standing or dependability.' He added, 'We have only one real currency in the USA [...] It is called the United States Dollar!'

On 16 and 17 July 2019, David Marcus was summoned before the US Congress for two excruciating days of grilling on all the different ways Libra would be a disaster. In October, it was Facebook CEO Mark Zuckerberg's turn in the hot seat before the House Committee on Financial Services Committee.

Governmental objections to Libra ranged from the mundane to the existential. At the most basic level, legislators wanted guarantees that Libra – unlike open-source cryptocurrencies – would indeed be censorable, and that the Libra Association would be able to block transactions involving money-laundering, terrorism financing or tax evasion. But Libra was also seen as a systemic risk: were it really to catch on among Facebook's users, it would become a currency serving one-third of the world's population, and just one cyber-security incident or 'Libra run'[5] away from disaster – potentially requiring national governments to bail it out. And there were serious questions about Libra's effect on national monetary policy, with fears[6] that Facebook's online parallel currency would render central banks unable to control the money supply effectively in their countries.

Under pressure from all sides, the Libra Association started haemorrhaging members: likely discomfited by the political uproar, PayPal was the first to jump ship in early October 2019. By the end of the month six other founding members – Booking Holdings, eBay, Mastercard, Mercado Pago, Stripe and Visa – had pulled out of the project.

In April 2020 the Libra Association – which eight months later would rebrand as 'Diem' – published a new, legalese-laden White Paper, manifestly the outcome of ten months of criticism, scolding and regulatory threats. Libra's launch had been pushed back to 2021, and its mission had changed: where the original White Paper had announced that Libra's goal was 'a stable currency' or 'a simple global currency', the new one wanted to create 'a simple global payment system'.

The 'basket'-backed Libra coin had taken a back seat to four new tokens pegged to national currencies – the US dollar, the Singapore dollar, the euro and the British pound sterling. As for the original Libra, it was now defined as 'a digital composite of some of the single-currency stablecoins', whose usage would be limited to cross-border transfers only. Gone was the promise to make the network permissionless over time, as a stricter compliance and vetting framework had been adopted. One line on page 11 pledged to work alongside central banks; 'Our hope is that as central banks develop central bank digital currencies (CBDCs), these CBDCs could be directly integrated with the Libra network.'

# The wake-up call

By January 2020, 80 per cent[7] of central banks worldwide were engaged in some kind of work or research on CBDC – a 10 per cent increase from just a year earlier. Monetary authorities had been exploring the concept for decades: it is essentially the idea of allowing citizens to open a digital account directly with central banks rather than forcing them to turn to commercial banks. Reasons to do so range from reducing banking fees, to helping people who do not have access to banking services to still use electronic payments from their phones, to implementing monetary policy without going through commercial banks. In a world where an increasing percentage of people engage in economic activity while barely touching cash, central banks that keep focusing only on printing notes start to feel anachronistic.

But the renewed interest in the technology certainly seems to have to do with the rise of stablecoins, and in particular with the announcement of Libra. The Bank for International Settlements – an international organisation of central bankers – attempted to put that narrative to sleep in June 2020, with a paper swearing that 'CBDC issuance is not so much a reaction to cryptocurrencies and private sector "stablecoin" proposals, but rather a focused technological effort by central banks to pursue several public policy objectives at once.' But that jars with common sense, and with what several central bankers have been saying since June 2019.

A March 2020 study by the Bank of England, the UK's central bank, listed[8] 'avoid[ing] the risks of new forms of private money creation, such as stablecoins' among the possible benefits of CBDC. Six months later the Bank's governor Andrew Bailey wondered, in a speech touching on the subject of stablecoins, whether 'a better outcome would be for central banks themselves to harness much of the technological and IT systems innovation and directly digitise cash?' He added that CBDC and stablecoins would not necessarily have to be mutually exclusive.

Every time a high-ranking official mentions 'stablecoins', it is safe to assume that is a byword for Libra, rather than for Maker DAO or any other DeFi venture. A report on stablecoins published by the Financial Action Task Force,[9] a G7-backed organisation fighting money-laundering, argues that decentralised stablecoins will likely never be widespread enough to pose a significant threat. 'Governments became scared of Libra,' says Jaya Klara Brekke, the Durham University scholar. 'Nothing else in cryptocurrency was really threatening: those were just little cute experiments and governments could watch and see how things might develop.'

All major economies' central banks – from the US Federal Reserve to the European Central Bank to the Bank of England – are currently looking into CBDC, even if none of them has yet outlined concrete plans or a precise roadmap. The only country that has already reached a partial roll-out phase is China.

As of August 2020, China's CBDC, called Digital Currency Electronic Payment (DCEP), was being piloted[10] in four major cities and three key industrial regions. It works on a mobile wallet app that can be used to pay in shops, or to transfer money directly wallet-to-wallet without relying on a bank's intermediation. The analogies with cryptocurrencies end there. The system is centralised, proprietary and, at its core, a tool for control: users' wallets are not anonymous, and the People's Bank of China can keep tabs on every single transaction – contributing to China's burgeoning surveillance state.

The development that Libra triggered is an interesting one. By aping the grammar of stablecoins, it has pushed governments – to wit, central banks, the cypherpunks' literal nemesis – to adopt the style and the outer trappings of cryptocurrencies. But the result cannot be anything other than a carnival-mirror version of Bitcoin and the others. 'The thing about Central Bank Digital Currency is: the most efficient system is in fact a central database,' says Michael Mainelli, an emeritus professor of commerce at the Gresham College and chairman of financial think tank Z/Yen. 'It's unlikely we're going to be doing anything like a cryptocurrency.'

Interestingly, however, if widespread adoption of CBDC ever comes to pass, one of its consequences will be more financial disintermediation. 'It will start a genuine debate about the rule of normal traditional banks in a fractional reserve banking system,' Mainelli says. '"I'm from the Bank of England. We got a new digital currency. You can use it on your phone, you know, good stuff. Oh, by the way, would you mind taking all of your CBDC and kindly putting it into Barclays or Santander, or somebody?" That could start a really intriguing discussion.'

# Epilogue: Cryptopias

---

Cryptocurrency was born as a political project. It emerged from obscure mailing lists and libertarian online forums, blending Austrian economics and computer science, gesturing towards a promised land of individual-to-individual interactions, no middlemen, and governments unable to stop dirty money or fleeing capitals flowing through the internet. That was always the ambition, even if the facts – and the technical implementations – often told a more nuanced tale.

Today a lot of that risks being lost in the noise. Big tech and central banks are locked in a standoff that might result in digital cash flooding everyone's phone. Bitcoin is an asset hoarded by high-flying financiers congregating in Swiss hamlets, and in the same breath governments are stiffening their stances, as in the case of the US and the UK's crackdown on cryptocurrency derivative trading.[1]

Online scams involving cryptocurrency happen almost daily, with a July 2020 heist involving the hijacking of 130 high-calibre Twitter accounts (including Elon Musk's, Joe Biden's and Barack Obama's) standing out for its boldness. New tokens are minted every day, always dancing on the line between shitcoin and useful technology. Game-theory-proofed financial constructs have taken over the blockchain. The yen for decentralisation and dis-intermediation might still be there, but it is often covered in a patina of *Wolf of Wall Street*-esque insouciance. The growing interest in Bitcoin from institutional investors and big businesses like car maker Tesla – which in February 2021 bought $1.5 billion in bitcoins, and whose CEO Elon Musk is a vocal cryptocurrency champion on Twitter – is an exceptional development whose long-term consequences are still hard to assess. Well over a decade after Bitcoin's debut, is cryptocurrency still political?

The easy answer is to say yes and point to the alt-right, the American rebrand of white supremacism for the Trump age. In March 2017 alt-right leader Richard

Spencer did call Bitcoin 'the currency of the alt right'. A few months later, following the Unite the Right Rally in Charlottesville, Virginia – when tiki-torch-toting thugs marched across the town intoning, 'Jews will not replace us', and a far-right activist murdered a left-wing counter-protester – Bitcoin donations to far-right organisations and individuals spiked, according to data from blockchain analytics firm Chainalysis. That has persisted to the present day. Between May 2014 and May 2020, Chainalysis figures found, neo-Nazi website the Daily Stormer had received the equivalent of more than $280,000 – most of it funnelled through gambling sites.[2]

But it is hard to disentangle ideological affinities from sheer convenience. The ultra-libertarian economics and mistrust of the Federal Reserve that inspired Bitcoin's creation might have been appealing to some members of the alt-right; it has even been suggested[3] that cryptocurrency's general anti-banker stance is rooted in anti-Semitic stereotypes and racism. Yet the alt-right's romance with cryptocurrency is more of a forced choice: as scrutiny around them has grown, mainstream payment processors like PayPal and Stripe started kicking alt-rightists and neo-Nazis off their platforms at an increasing rate. Bitcoin has become by necessity the only way the alt-right could receive donations – exactly like criminals or Islamic State terrorists.

To hear a (slightly) more articulate political vision hinging on cryptocurrency, however, one does not have to move too far along the political spectrum. In March 2018 Donald Trump's former chief strategist – and Brock Pierce's erstwhile business partner – Stephen K. Bannon took to a stage in Zurich and announced that he was launching a populist political movement along the lines of the Donald Trump and Brexit campaigns, and that cryptocurrency would lie at the heart of it.

'That new currency is going to empower this movement, empower companies, empower governments to get away from the central banks that debase your currency and make you what is slave wages – keep you on the spinning wheel of slaves to debt,' Bannon said.

Weeks later he revealed that he was in the process of building 'utility tokens for the populist movement', which would let his followers earn some kind of benefit in exchange for their political activism.[4] As of 2020, Bannon's ambition to create a Europe-wide nationalist group, called the Movement, had barely registered; no populist token has yet been launched.

Perhaps, however, neither the alt-right's Richard Spencer nor Bannon should be regarded as significant – if anything, because they have barely any idea of what they are dealing with: they cannot fully appreciate the technology's potential because they cannot design and work with the technology themselves. For crypto-politics to take off in this sphere, its architects will have to come from *within* the field of cryptocurrency.

As of today, there are two main candidates who fit that bill.

One is Amir Taaki,[5] a British Bitcoin developer who over the last few years has transmogrified into a Garibaldi-esque character, touring the world to support freedom fighters. In 2015 Taaki left the UK for Rojava, a Kurdish-controlled autonomous region in Northern Syria. He joined the Kurds, started fighting against the Islamic State insurgence, and became learned in the thinking of Kurdish political leader Abdullah Öcalan. He embraced Öcalan's democratic confederalism – a doctrine that rejects the idea of nation state and promotes the emergence of self-governing, environmentalist, feminist, direct-democratic local communities – and became persuaded that Bitcoin could help bring it about across the globe.

Taaki returned to Europe in 2017 and despaired at the sight of Bitcoin's transformation into the plaything of day-traders and scammers. He therefore decided to focus his efforts on giving Bitcoin a sense of purpose. He decamped to Barcelona – the capital of a Catalonia that was still reeling from recent pro-independence turmoil and the subsequent clamp down by the Spanish government – and started putting together a collective of technologists devoted to building the tools for revolution: anonymous cryptocurrency wallets and blockchain-based messaging systems, alongside non-cryptocurrency technology applications. The initiative, which Taaki christened Autonomous Polytechnics, is still at the work-in-progress stage, but it is doubtless one of the most intriguing blueprints for a cryptocurrency-fuelled political future in existence today.

The other major contender in the arena is Vitalik Buterin. For half a decade Ethereum's benevolent dictator has been grappling with issues of political design, wielding cryptoeconomics to fine-tune a platform that could remain decentralised and in the same breath minimise the occurrence of the DAO-grade catastrophes. It was almost inevitable that all that would eventually be parlayed into some kind of political theory.

In 2018 that became official. On his Medium blog,[6] Buterin announced the start of an intellectual partnership with economist and academic Glen Weyl, who was famous for advocating a theory dubbed 'liberal radicalism': the idea that free-market principles should be taken to the extremes and usher in a quasi-abolition of private property.

In a book he co-authored, *Radical Markets*, Weyl proposes to transform society into a perennial auction: people should set a price for each of their possessions and be ready to sell it to whoever comes forward bidding for it. People setting too high a price will be slapped with mammoth wealth taxes, to be redistributed among the citizenry. This process, Weyl believes, would wind up rebalancing inequalities and would hopefully break down the centralised monopolies that have a stranglehold on the global economy.

Weyl even proposes applying this market logic to democracy. The 'one person, one vote' set-up should be ditched in favour of a mechanism called 'quadratic voting', in which each voter is allotted a certain amount of voting credits that can be hoarded or sold. This way, people who really care about the outcome of a certain vote can cast several ballots in one go.

Weyl's ideas might sound exciting, but they are a hard sell in most Western democracies. Still, some of the rules and governance concepts included in *Radical Markets* could be easily programmed and tried out in blockchain communities such as Ethereum – which is why Weyl and Buterin started working together.

The outcome of that collaboration is an organisation called RadicalxChange, whose goals include quadratic voting, constant auctioning and radical anti-trust measures. In a speech at the organisation's yearly conference in July 2019,[7] Buterin sketched out an intellectual history of cryptocurrency from the early cypherpunks to the DAO debacle. The main takeaway was that cypherpunks' fondness for hardcore individualism could not survive impact with the inescapable fact that currency – including cryptocurrency – is a social construct enforced by a community and steered by governance. There was more: Buterin suggested that cryptocurrency and blockchain technologies – coupled with Weyl's ideas – might help effect meaningful change in a world ravaged by inequality and increasingly tempted to turn to populism. That was quite a reversal for a technology first sought by libertarians in search of an emergency exit from the offline world to a government-free cyberspace. Can Buterin redefine what cryptocurrency means?

Hard to tell. Cryptocurrency has been constantly evolving since its inception, in Satoshi Nakamoto's White Paper. It went from coding experiment to multibillion sensation, from slow payments to smart contracts, from scam to coveted asset, from public enemy to blueprint for central banks. Whether cryptocurrency will go on to become an instrument for alt-right extremism, for firebrand revolutionary projects or for blue-sky utopianism, no one can fathom yet. Maybe it will go in all those directions, the way blockchains split to pursue different destinies; maybe it will go nowhere.

But do you still doubt that cryptocurrency is a political project?

# Glossary

**Bitcoin**

The first open-source decentralised cryptocurrency, proposed by Satoshi Nakamoto in 2008 and launched the following year. It kick-started the cryptocurrency industry and remains the most highly priced cryptocurrency, as of 2020.

**Bitcoin maximalist**

A cryptocurrency adherent maintaining that Bitcoin is the only legitimate cryptocurrency.

**Blockchain**

The decentralised online network on which cryptocurrency is exchanged. It is a ledger of all the transactions that ever took place in a given cryptocurrency, stacked in discrete chunks or 'blocks', and collectively updated by independent servers – or nodes – via a cryptographic process.

### CBDC (Central Bank Digital Currency)

A kind of digital money issued directly by central banks, which would allow users to access electronic payments while bypassing commercial banks. Largely considered a reaction to cryptocurrency's increasing prominence.

### Cryptocurrency

A technology enabling the exchange of digital units of value with the aid of cryptographic techniques. It was envisioned by the Cypherpunks as a payment system that could not be blocked or interfered with by governments or law enforcement; that goal requires the system to be decentralised rather than run by a single entity.

### Cryptocurrency exchange

A company that allows users to exchange legal tender (such as dollars, euros or pounds) for cryptocurrency and vice versa, or to exchange cryptocurrencies for other cryptocurrencies. The price of a given cryptocurrency in legal tender is determined by demand for – and supply of – it on the exchange, which sometimes leads to speculators arbitraging between exchanges.

### Cypherpunks

A group of libertarian technologists congregating in Silicon Valley in the 1990s, and then on the Cypherpunks mailing list. They believed in the importance of strong privacy technology, including cryptocurrency.

### DAO (Decentralised Autonomous Organisation)

A cluster of self-executing programs built on top of a blockchain, which provide a service to users and possibly revenue to its shareholders, ostensibly with minimal or no human management. Sometimes called a DAC (Decentralised Autonomous Corporation). Not to be mistaken for The DAO, a disgraced DAO launched – and immediately hacked – in 2016.

### DAPP

An online application built on a blockchain.

### DeFi (Decentralised Finance)

An emerging breed of applications built on the Ethereum blockchain, with the aim of creating a decentralised alternative to traditional financial services – including loans, escrows, derivatives and exchanges.

### Disintermediation

The removal of 'middlemen' from economic transactions, one of the stated goals of cryptocurrency and blockchain.

### Ether

The cryptocurrency that powers the Ethereum blockchain, where it is used for payments or carrying out other operations.

### Ethereum

A blockchain that enables developers to create 'smart contracts' – that is, self-enforcing routines that activate in response to a payment or transaction.

### 51% attack

A type of blockchain hack predicated on deploying enough computing power to take over the majority of mining nodes, and then approving invalid transactions.

### Flash loan

A kind of loan available from some DeFi services, allowing investors to take a loan without providing any collateral, as long as the loaned sum is returned almost immediately.

## Hard fork

A blockchain's bifurcation, triggered by a change to the underlying protocol. It often results in a schism between groups of users each choosing a different path forward.

## Hash

A string of digits of a standard length, able to uniquely represent any piece of information (a sentence, a file, an image, etc). Hashes are widely used in cryptography.

## Hodl

Originally a misspelling of 'hold', this has become a popular motto in cryptocurrency circles, inciting investors to hold on to their cryptocurrency troves, in the hope that their price will skyrocket.

## ICO (Initial Coin Offering)

The online auctioning of cryptocurrency tokens to the public, often with the promise of investing the funds from the auction in the development of a blockchain where the tokens can be spent to access a service. Increasingly rare, owing to regulatory issues and the prevalence of scams.

### Libra

A cryptocurrency pegged to a 'basket' of fiat currencies and bonds, proposed by Facebook and other companies in June 2019. Governmental backlash forced a redesign of its blueprint. Rebranded as 'Diem' in December 2020.

### Miner

A person, company or pool of individuals using specialised computer equipment to run a blockchain's node and validate cryptocurrency transactions, receiving a reward in newly minted (mined) cryptocurrency units or fees from transactions. Usually the term is only applied to proof-of-work systems; in the other cases, 'validator' is used.

### Premined

Cryptocurrency that is not created through mining – like Bitcoin is – but sold to users in an ICO or other distribution event.

### Proof-of-stake

A technique that requires a blockchain's validators to stake a certain amount of cryptocurrency in order to approve transactions, under penalty of losing it if they incorrectly wave through invalid transactions.

## Proof-of-work

A mining technique that requires miners to solve a time- and energy-consuming mathematical puzzle in order to validate transactions and create new blocks. The puzzle's difficulty increases over time, meaning that mining requires more and more spending on computing equipment and energy costs.

## Satoshi Nakamoto

The pseudonymous inventor of Bitcoin, whose real identity or whereabouts remain unknown. It is unclear whether Satoshi Nakamoto is a man, a woman or a group of people. A 'satoshi' is also the name of a sub-unit of Bitcoin, equivalent to one-hundred-millionth of a Bitcoin.

## Shitcoin

A derogatory term for cryptocurrency tokens with no apparent value or utility, often sold in dubious ICOs.

### Smart contract

A self-enforcing program powered by cryptocurrency transactions, proposed by Cypherpunk Nick Szabo and first implemented on Ethereum.

### Stablecoin

A cryptocurrency whose price is not determined by supply and demand, but is pegged – in various ways – to that of a legal tender, thus reducing cryptocurrency's infamous volatility.

### Tether

The most widely used stablecoin, whose value is theoretically pegged one-to-one to the US dollar. It is run in a centralised way by a company that originally claimed to have enough dollar reserves to redeem all the tether coins in circulation.

### Token

A unit of cryptocurrency, in some cases designed for purposes other than economic transactions.

**Trustless**

A system whose smooth functioning and honesty do not depend on any one individual's good conduct, but are ensured by the system's very architecture. Blockchain-based systems are (somehow simplistically) called 'trustless', in that their operations are ostensibly governed by publicly known computer code rather than potentially corrupt human agents.

**Wallet**

A pair of cryptographic codes – contained in an app, a computer programme, or a piece of hardware – that allow a user to spend and receive cryptocurrency. Enthusiasts often rely on 'custodial wallets', in which their keys are actually stored by a third party – usually an exchange.

**White Paper**

A document, usually a PDF file, proposing a new cryptocurrency project. The first was Satoshi Nakamoto's 'Bitcoin: A Peer-to-Peer Electronic Cash System', also known simply as the Bitcoin White Paper.

## Yield farming

A DeFi trend that allows investors to earn new tokens by depositing cryptocurrencies on decentralised lending markets.

# Acknowledgements

I started writing this book just as London, alongside most of Europe, was sliding into a lockdown in order to confront the novel coronavirus pandemic. Like many others, overcome by the ennui of spending weeks and weeks at home, I took up baking: every week I would commandeer the kitchen and knead enormous slabs of focaccia. For me, memories about writing this book will forever be intertwined with the smell of rosemary, and with the sound of my frenzied chomping on vast chunks of oily focaccia while striving to find the right word to explain a technical concept. I am very grateful to that focaccia; I am also grateful to my then-housemate, Gianfranco, for reacting with just a hint of puzzlement towards my literary-culinary antics.

But of course my gratitude goes first and foremost to the *WIRED UK* team, and in particular to *WIRED*'s editor Greg Williams, for giving me the opportunity to try my hand at writing a book on a topic that I love and dread at once. And to Penguin's Nigel Wilcockson, whose suggestions, remarks and edits never failed to improve what I had written.

Thanks to the experts, researchers, entrepreneurs and developers who were interviewed for this book. Whether they ended up being quoted or not, they all were instrumental in shaping how the book turned out.

I also need to thank the many others who have helped me throughout these long (well, they felt long) months, offering comments on my various drafts. Thanks to Ioiana, Chris, Akram, Alessandro, Dom and my brother Edoardo. You really helped – if anything, by reassuring me that what I was writing was not utterly unintelligible.

Special shout-outs to Fiorenzo Manganiello for his insightful observations; to Harry Halpin, who was always ready to provide staggeringly crystal-clear explanations of some of the most intricate concepts in this field; and to Chainalysis's Philip Gradwell for his pithy description of how cryptocurrency transactions can be – and are – investigated.

Finally, thanks to my family, because *la famiglia prima di tutto*. Thanks to Antolo for the Frisbee sessions. To Hideo Kojima, Neil Druckmann and Rockstar Games, whose masterpieces prevented me from completely freaking out in the midst of a focaccia-filled book-writing pandemic.

And thanks to the thinkers, tinkerers, chancers, fraudsters, speculators, utopians, podcasters, bloggers, hackers, criminals, developers, engineers, inventors, cypherpunks, fighters and libertarians who have created, and keep creating, cryptocurrency in all its forms. The world would be too boring a place without you. Keep aiming for the Moon.

# Notes

Notes to 1 Bitcoin                    pages 5–42

1   May, T. C., 1992, 'The Crypto Anarchist Manifesto', Activism. net. Available at: https://www.activism.net/cypherpunk/ crypto-anarchy.html (accessed 17 October 2020)

2   May, T. C.,1994, 'THE CYPHERNOMICON: Cypherpunks FAQ and More, Version 0.666', Cypherpunks.to. Available at: https://web.archive.org/web/20160809001639/http:// www.cypherpunks.to/faq/cyphernomicron/chapter4. html#2 (accessed 17 October 2020)

3   Cryptoanarchy.wiki, n.d., 'Notable Posters (First Name A–Z)'. Available at: https://mailing-list-archive. cryptoanarchy.wiki/authors/notable/ (accessed 17 October 2020)

4   May, T., 1997, 'Untraceable Digital Cash, Information Markets, and BlackNet', *The Seventh Conference on Computers, Freedom, and Privacy*, Burlingame, CA.

Available at: http://osaka.law.miami.edu/~froomkin/ articles/tcmay.htm (accessed 17 October 2020)

5   Hughes, E., 2020, 'Eric Hughes: A Cypherpunk's Manifesto', Bitcoin News. Available at: https://news.bitcoin.com/eric-hughes-a-cypherpunks-manifesto/ (accessed 17 October 2020)

6   Brunton, F., *Digital Cash: The Unknown History of the Anarchists, Utopians, and Technologists Who Created Cryptocurrency* (Princeton University Press, 2019)

7   Hayek, F., *Denationalization of Money* (Inst. of Economic Affairs, 1978)

8   Chaum, D., 'Blind Signatures for Untraceable Payments', in Chaum, D., Rivest, R. L. and Sherman, A. T. (eds), *Advances in Cryptology* (Springer, 1983)

9   Wei Dai, 2020, 'Bmoney', Weidai.com. Available at: http://www.weidai.com/bmoney.txt (accessed 17 October 2020)

10  LaFrance, A., 2020, 'The Prophecies of Q', *The Atlantic*. Available at: https://www.theatlantic.com/magazine/archive/2020/06/qanon-nothing-can-stop-what-is-coming/610567/ (accessed 17 October 2020)

11    Nakamoto, S., 2008, 'Bitcoin: A Peer-To-Peer Electronic
      Cash System'. Available at: https://bitcoin.org/bitcoin.pdf
      (accessed 17 October 2020)

12    Blockchain.news, 2020, 'Satoshi Nakamoto's Quotes
      on Trust – Trusted Third Parties'. Available at: https://
      blockchain.news/wiki/satoshi-nakamotos-quotes-on-
      trust-trusted-third-parties (accessed 17 October 2020)

13    Satoshi.nakamotoinstitute.org, n.d., 'Bitcoin P2P E-Cash
      Paper', Satoshi Nakamoto Institute. Available at: https://
      satoshi.nakamotoinstitute.org/emails/cryptography/
      12/#selection-89.0–89.126 (accessed 17 October 2020)

14    Nakamoto, S., Bridle, J., Brekke, J. and Vickers, B., *The
      White Paper* (Ignota, 2019)

15    The word, initially rendered as 'block chain', would be
      coined by cypherpunk and Cryptography subscriber
      Hal Finney in an email exchange with Nakamoto
      (see: https://satoshi.nakamotoinstitute.org/emails/
      cryptography/6/)

16    Satoshi.nakamotoinstitute.org, n.d., 'Bitcoin Does NOT
      Violate Mises' Regression Theorem', Satoshi Nakamoto

Institute. Available at: https://satoshi.nakamotoinstitute.org/posts/bitcointalk/threads/137/ (accessed 17 October 2020)

17   Metzdowd.com, n.d., 'ADMIN: End of Bitcoin Discussion for Now'. Available at: https://www.metzdowd.com/pipermail/cryptography/2008-November/014867.html (accessed 17 October 2020)

18   Of course the obverse of disintermediation is 'reintermediation': a handful of platforms emerge as the main channels where those peer-to-peer relationships play out; the fall of middlemen makes room for the rise of winner-takes-all giants. In the internet domain, Amazon and Airbnb are the obvious examples. On the Bitcoin network, that scenario should be staved off by wedding disintermediation with decentralisation, thus replacing dominant platforms with a scattered network where no one is in command. (Whether that can be attained in practice is a matter of debate.)

19   Thomas, K., 2010, 'Could the Wikileaks Scandal Lead to New Virtual Currency?', *PC World*. Available at: https://www.pcworld.com/article/213230/could_wikileaks_scandal_lead_to_new_virtual_currency.html (accessed 17 October 2020)

20   See: https://web.archive.org/web/20201017154256/https://
     twitter.com/wikileaks/status/80774521350668288

21   Gerlach, J., Demos, G. and Sornette, D., 2019, 'Dissection
     of Bitcoin's multiscale bubble history from January 2012
     to February 2018', *Royal Society Open Science*, 6 (7),
     p.180643

22   Baur, D., Hong, K. and Lee, A., 2018, 'Bitcoin: Medium
     of exchange or speculative assets?', *Journal of
     International Financial Markets, Institutions and Money*,
     54, pp. 177–89

23   *LSE Business Review*, 2020, 'Why Economists Are Relaxed
     About Bitcoin'. Available at: https://blogs.lse.ac.uk/
     businessreview/2017/12/20/why-economists-are-relaxed-
     about-bitcoin/ (accessed 17 October 2020)

24   TokenAnalyst Team, 2020, 'Centralisation In Bitcoin
     Mining: A Data-Driven Investigation', *Medium*. Available
     at: https://medium.com/tokenanalyst/centralisation-in-
     bitcoin-mining-a-data-driven-investigation-7fb0caa48157
     (accessed 17 October 2020)

Notes to 2 Ethereum                                    pages 43–74

1    Matzutt, R., Hiller, J., Henze, M., Ziegeldorf, J., Müllmann,
     D., Hohlfeld, O. and Wehrle, K., 2018, 'A Quantitative
     Analysis of the Impact of Arbitrary Blockchain Content
     on Bitcoin', *Financial Cryptography and Data Security*,
     pp. 420–38

2    Buterin, V., n.d., 'Vitalik Buterin on About.Me', about.me.
     Available at: https://about.me/vitalik_buterin (accessed
     17 October 2020)

3    Buterin, V., 2020, 'Bitcoin Adoption Opportunity:
     Teenagers', *Bitcoin Magazine*. Available at: https://
     bitcoinmagazine.com/articles/bitcoin-adoption-
     opportunity-teenager-1330407280 (accessed
     17 October 2020)

4    Szabo, N., 1996, 'Nick Szabo – Smart Contracts:
     Building Blocks for Digital Markets', Fon.hum.uva.
     nl. Available at: https://www.fon.hum.uva.nl/rob/
     Courses/InformationInSpeech/CDROM/Literature/
     LOTwinterschool2006/szabo.best.vwh.net/smart_
     contracts_2.html (accessed 17 October 2020)

5   That is a reference to the 'Turing machine', a hypothetical
    computer – posited by British computer scientist Alan
    Turing – able to process every possible computable problem.

6   Wood, G., 2014, *Ethereum: A Secure Decentralised
    Generalised Transaction Ledger*, Ethereum project
    Yellow Paper, 151 (2014), pp.1–32. Available at: https://
    ethereum.github.io/yellowpaper/paper.pdf (accessed
    1 February 2021)

7   Wood, G., 2020, 'Đapps: What Web 3.0 Looks Like',
    Gavwood.com. Available at: http://gavwood.com/
    dappsweb3.html (accessed 17 October 2020)

8   2017, *Decentralizing Everything with Ethereum's Vitalik
    Buterin, Disrupt SF 2017* [video]. Available at: https://
    www.youtube.com/watch?v=WSN5BaCzsbo (accessed
    17 October 2020)

9   Russo, C., 2020, 'Sale of the Century: The Inside Story of
    Ethereum's 2014 Premine – Coindesk', CoinDesk. Available
    at: https://www.coindesk.com/sale-of-the-century-the-
    inside-story-of-ethereums-2014-premine (accessed
    17 October 2020)

10 That is not to say that mining does not produce Ether: it does. But as of 2020, the amount of Ether that mining has injected into the system is lower than that sold back in 2014. That is by design: even if Ether does not have a fixed cap – e.g. Bitcoin's 21 million – it can only produce up to a certain number of ethers every year.

11 Bitcointalk.org, 2020, '[ETH] Ethereum = Scam'. Available at: https://bitcointalk.org/index.php?topic=707237.20 (accessed 17 October 2020)

12 See: https://web.archive.org/web/20201017160534/https://twitter.com/adam3us/status/1291298850301513730?s=19

13 Larimer, D., 2020, 'Overpaying For Security', Let's Talk Bitcoin. Available at: https://letstalkbitcoin.com/is-bitcoin-overpaying-for-false-security (accessed 17 October 2020)

14 Sheldonth.com, n.d. Available at: http://sheldonth.com/static/Mike%20Hearn%2CAgents.mp4 (accessed 17 October 2020)

15 In fact, the concept of the 'ownerless' company had already been proposed, without the cryptocurrency element, by Berkeley legal scholar Meir Dan-Cohen back in 1986

(see: Bell, R. and Dan-Cohen, M., 1987, 'Rights, Persons, and Organizations: A Legal Theory for Bureaucratic Society', *Contemporary Sociology*, 16 (3), p. 320)

16   GitHub, 2016, 'Blockchainsllc/DAO'. Available at: https://github.com/blockchainsllc/DAO (accessed 17 October 2020])

17   Jentzsch, C., 2016, 'The History of The DAO and Lessons Learned', *Medium*. Available at: https://blog.slock.it/the-history-of-the-dao-and-lessons-learned-d06740f8cfa5 (accessed 17 October 2020)

18   *Economist*, 2020, 'The DAO of Accrue'. Available at: https://www.economist.com/finance-and-economics/2016/05/19/the-dao-of-accrue (accessed 17 October 2020)

19   De Filippi, P. and Wright, A., *Blockchain and the Law* (Harvard University Press, 2019)

20   Gün Sirer, E., 2016, 'Thoughts on The DAO Hack', *Hacking Distributed*. Available at: https://hackingdistributed.com/2016/06/17/thoughts-on-the-dao-hack/ (accessed 17 October 2020)

21  Todd, P., 2016, 'The Ethereum DAO Bailout Needs a Coin
    Vote', Petertodd.org. Available at: https://petertodd.
    org/2016/ethereum-dao-bailout-vote#fn:earlyhardforks
    (accessed 17 October 2020)

22  Zamfir, V., 2019, 'Against Szabo's Law, For a New Crypto
    Legal System', *Medium*. Available at: https://medium.com/
    cryptolawreview/against-szabos-law-for-a-new-crypto-
    legal-system-d00d0f3d3827 (accessed 17 October 2020)

## Notes to 3 The ICO bubble                  pages 75–99

1   See: http://web.archive.org/save/https://www.linkedin.
    com/in/jrwillett/

2   2013, '42. BITCOIN 2013 – Day 2 – Bitcoin in the Future,
    Part 4 of 5', YouTube. Available at: https://www.youtube.
    com/watch?time_continue=335&v=4bMf4xZg_4U&feature
    =emb_logo (accessed 17 October 2020)

3   Volpicelli, G., 2017, 'The $3.8Bn Cryptocurrency Bubble Is a
    Huge Deal. But It Could Break the Blockchain', *WIRED UK*.
    Available at: https://www.wired.co.uk/article/what-is-initial-
    coin-offering-ico-token-sale (accessed 17 October 2020)

4    Shifflett, S., 2018, 'A Flood of Questionable Cryptocurrency Offerings', *Wall Street Journal*. Available at: https://www. wsj.com/graphics/whitepapers/ (accessed 17 October 2020)

5    Fenu, G., Marchesi, L., Marchesi, M. and Tonelli, R., March 2018, 'The ICO phenomenon and its relationships with ethereum smart contract environment', in IEEE, *2018 International Workshop on Blockchain Oriented Software Engineering (IWBOSE)*, pp. 26–32

6    EY, 2017, 'EY Research: Initial Coin Offerings (ICOs)'. Available at: https://web.archive.org/ web/20180710094813/https://www.ey.com/Publication/ vwLUAssets/ey-research-initial-coin-offerings- icos/%24File/ey-research-initial-coin-offerings-icos.pdf (accessed 17 October 2020)

7    Floyd Mayweather Jr, Paris Hilton, Jamie Foxx and Luis Suárez are just some of the best-known celebrities who promoted ICOs.

8    Buterin, V., 2017, 'Analyzing Token Sale Models', Vitalik.ca. Available at: https://vitalik.ca/general/2017/06/09/sales. html (accessed 17 October 2020)

9    Alois, J., 2019, 'SEC Freezes $8 Million from Alleged Bogus ICO & Manipulation Fraud Perpetrated by Reggie Middleton [U]', Crowdfund Insider. Available at: https://www.crowdfundinsider.com/2019/08/150540-sec-freezes-8-million-from-alleged-bogus-ico-manipulation-fraud-perpetrated-by-reggie-middleton/ (accessed 17 October 2020)

10   Kharpal, A., 2017, 'Initial Coin Offerings Have Raised $1.2 Billion and Now Surpass Early Stage VC Funding', CNBC. Available at: https://www.cnbc.com/2017/08/09/initial-coin-offerings-surpass-early-stage-venture-capital-funding.html (accessed 17 October 2020)

11   Benedetti, H. and Kostovetsky, L., 2018, 'Digital Tulips? Returns to Investors in Initial Coin Offerings', *SSRN Electronic Journal*.

12   See Chapter Two.

13   Volpicelli, G., 2018, 'To Get Rich in Crypto You Just Need an Idea, and a Coin', *WIRED UK*. Available at: https://www.wired.co.uk/article/ico-bitcoin-blockchain-cryptocurrency-bubble (accessed 17 October 2020)

14 Bullock, N., 2018, 'Blockchain Start-Up Raises More than $4Bn', *Financial Times*. Available at: https://www.ft.com/ content/69abdb66-666c-11e8-b6eb-4acfcfb08c11 (accessed 17 October 2020)

15 EY, 2018, *EY study: Initial Coin Offerings (ICOs) The Class of 2017 – one year later.* Available at: https://web. archive.org/web/20200930175629/https://www.ey.com/ Publication/vwLUAssets/ey-study-ico-research/%24FILE/ ey-study-ico-research.pdf (accessed 17 October 2020)

16 Dead Coins, n.d., 'List'. Available at: https://deadcoins.com/ (accessed 17 October 2020)

17 Securities and Exchange Commission, 2018, 'Report of Investigation Pursuant to Section 21(a) of the Securities Exchange Act of 1934: The DAO'. Available at: https://www. sec.gov/litigation/investreport/34-81207.pdf (accessed 17 October 2020)

18 Kik Interactive, Inc., 2017, *Kin: A Decentralized Ecosystem of Digital Services for Daily Life* [e-book]. Available at: https://www.kin.org/static/files/Kin_Whitepaper_V1_ English.pdf (accessed 17 October 2020)

19  Securities and Exchange Commission, 2019, 'Re: Cipher Technologies Bitcoin Fund Registration Statement on Form N-2 (Filed 13 May 2019) Pre-Effective Amendment No. 1 (Filed 11 Sept. 2019) File No. 811-23443'. Available at: https://www.sec.gov/Archives/edgar/data/1776589/999999999719007180/filename1.pdf (accessed 2 February 2021)

20  Securities and Exchange Commission, 2019, 'SEC Charges Issuer with Conducting $100 Million Unregistered ICO'. Available at: https://www.sec.gov/news/press-release/2019-87 (accessed 17 October 2020)

21  Livingston, T., 2019, 'Moving Forward Boldly with Kin', *Medium*. Available at: https://medium.com/@tedlivingston/moving-forward-boldly-with-kin-ec6290a6453 (accessed 17 October 2020)

22  Patterson, M., 2018, 'Crypto's 80% Plunge Is Now Worse than the Dot-Com Crash', Bloomberg.com. Available at: https://www.bloomberg.com/news/articles/2018-09-12/crypto-s-crash-just-surpassed-dot-com-levels-as-losses-reach-80 (accessed 17 October 2020)

23   PwC, 2020, *6th ICO / STO Report*, PwC. Available at:
     https://www.pwc.ch/en/insights/fs/6th-ico-sto-report.
     html (accessed 17 October 2020)

24   Williams-Grut, O., 2018, 'Startups Raised $5.6 Billion
     Through Icos in 2017 – Insider', *Insider*. Available
     at: https://amp.insider.com/how-much-raised-icos-
     2017-tokendata-2017–2018-1 (accessed 17 October
     2020)

25   EY, 2018, 'ICO Portfolio Is Down by 66% in the First Half of
     2018, According to EY Study'. Available at: http://ey.com/
     en_kw/news/2018/10/i-c-o-portfolio-is-down-by-sixty-six-
     percent-in-the-first-half-according-to-ey-study (accessed
     17 October 2020)

## Notes to 4 Stablecoins and finance    pages 101–132

1    Schatzker, E., 2017, 'A Crypto Fund King Says Bitcoin Will
     Be the Biggest Bubble Ever', Bloomberg.com. Available at:
     https://www.bloomberg.com/news/articles/2017–09-26/
     mike-novogratz-is-set-for-comeback-with-crytocurrency-
     hedge-fund (accessed 17 October 2020)

2   Tether Limited, 2016, 'Tether: Fiat Currencies on the
    Bitcoin Blockchain'. Available at: https://tether.to/wp-
    content/uploads/2016/06/TetherWhitePaper.pdf (accessed
    17 October 2020)

3   See: http://archive.is/ZFDBf

4   Chavkin, S., 2019, 'Paradise Papers Connection Sparks
    Massive Bitcoin Lawsuit – ICIJ', ICIJ. Available at: https://
    www.icij.org/investigations/paradise-papers/paradise-
    papers-connection-sparks-massive-bitcoin-lawsuit/
    (accessed 17 October 2020)

5   Griffin, J. and Shams, A., 2020, 'Is Bitcoin Really
    Untethered?', *Journal of Finance*, 75 (4),
    pp.1913–64

6   Cai, J., 2019, 'Data Analysis: Tether Manipulation Did Not
    Cause Bitcoin's 2017 Bull Run', longhash. Available at:
    https://www.longhash.com/en/news/3208/Data-Analysis:-
    Tether-Manipulation-Did-Not-Cause-Bitcoin%27s-2017-
    Bull-Run (accessed 17 October 2020)

7   'In re Tether and Bitfinex Crypto Asset Litigation [2020]
    Case 1:19-cv-09236-KPF' (United States District Court

Southern District of New York). Available at: https://www.courtlistener.com/recap/gov.uscourts.nysd.524076/gov.uscourts.nysd.524076.110.0.pdf (accessed 2 February 2021)

8     Courts.state.ny.us, 2020, 'Matter of James v iFinex Inc. (2020 NY Slip Op 03880)'. Available at: http://www.courts.state.ny.us/reporter/3dseries/2020/2020_03880.htm (accessed 17 October 2020)

9     Kharif, O., 2019, 'The World's Most-Used Cryptocurrency Isn't Bitcoin', Bloomberg.com. Available at: https://www.bloomberg.com/news/articles/2019–10-01/tether-not-bitcoin-likely-the-world-s-most-used-cryptocurrency (accessed 17 October 2020)

10    Blog.chainalysis.com, 2020, 'East Asia: Pro Traders and Stablecoins Drive World's Biggest Cryptocurrency Market'. Available at: https://blog.chainalysis.com/reports/east-asia-cryptocurrency-market-2020 (accessed 17 October 2020)

11    Dell'Erba, M., 2019, 'Stablecoins in Cryptoeconomics. From Initial Coin Offerings (ICOs) to Central Bank Digital Currencies (CBDCs)', *New York University Journal of*

*Legislation and Public Policy*. Available at: https://ssrn.com/abstract=3385840 (accessed 2 February 2021)

12   Tamuly, B., 2018, 'Stablecoin Space to Face Storm of Disruption from ROCKZ, a Coin Backed by One of the Strongest Currencies in the World', AMBCrypto. Available at: https://ambcrypto.com/stablecoin-space-to-face-storm-of-disruption-from-rockz-a-coin-backed-by-one-of-the-strongest-currencies-in-the-world/ (accessed 17 October 2020)

13   Sams, R., 2015, 'A Note on Cryptocurrency Stabilisation: Seigniorage Shares', 2nd version. Available at: https://blog.bitmex.com/wp-content/uploads/2018/06/A-Note-on-Cryptocurrency-Stabilisation-Seigniorage-Shares.pdf (accessed 17 October 2020)

14   Hileman, G., 2019, 'State of Stablecoins (2019)', *SSRN Electronic Journal*. Available at: http://dx.doi.org/10.2139/ssrn.3533143 (accessed 2 February 2021)

15   Consensys, 2020, 'Defi User Research Report'. Available at: https://pages.consensys.net/codefi-def-user-research-report (accessed 17 October 2020)

16    In fact something similar, although not existentially
      catastrophic, happened in March 2020. When the novel
      coronavirus crisis sent the prices of cryptocurrencies
      tumbling vertiginously, several Ether-filled Vaults on Maker
      DAO suddenly became under-collateralised. But with the
      whole Ethereum network in disarray as people scrambled
      to cash out their crypto savings, many of the liquidating
      auctions ended up with a single bidder – who offered exactly
      zero Dai in exchange for a lot of Ether, and won the auction.
      (A lawsuit against Maker DAO's Maker Foundation followed.)

## Notes to 5 Libra                    pages 133–151

1    Statista, 2020, 'Number of Blockchain Wallets 2020',
     Statista. Available at: https://www.statista.com/
     statistics/647374/worldwide-blockchain-wallet-users/
     (accessed 17 October 2020)

2    See: https://webcache.googleusercontent.com/search?q=c
     ache:5WEB0hMcU5cJ:https://twitter.com/musalbas/status
     /1143629828551270401%3Flang%3Den+&cd=2&hl=en&ct=c
     lnk&gl=uk

3    Tang, F., 2019, 'Will China Be Forced to Develop Its Own
     Cryptocurrency in Response to Libra?', *South China Morning
     Post*. Available at: https://www.scmp.com/economy/china-
     economy/article/3017716/facebooks-libra-forcing-china-
     step-plans-its-own (accessed 17 October 2020)

4    See: https://web.archive.org/web/20201017192854/
     https://twitter.com/realDonaldTrump/
     status/1149472284702208000

5    Pistor, K., 2019, 'Facebook's Libra Must Be Stopped –
     Katharina Pistor', Social Europe. Available at: https://
     www.socialeurope.eu/facebooks-libra-must-be-stopped
     (accessed 17 October 2020)

6    Greeley, B., 2019, 'Facebook's Libra Currency Is Wake-Up
     Call for Central Banks', *Financial Times*. Available at:
     https://www.ft.com/content/6960c7a4-f313-11e9-b018-
     3ef8794b17c6 (accessed 17 October 2020)

7    Bank for International Settlements, 2020, 'Impending
     Arrival – A Sequel to the Survey on Central Bank Digital
     Currency', BIS Papers No. 107. Available at: https://www.bis.
     org/publ/bppdf/bispap107.pdf (accessed 17 October 2020)

8    Bank of England, 2020, 'Central Bank Digital Currency: Opportunities, Challenges and Design'. Available at: https://www.bankofengland.co.uk/paper/2020/central-bank-digital-currency-opportunities-challenges-and-design-discussion-paper (accessed 17 October 2020)

9    Financial Action Task Force (FATF), 2020, 'FATF Report to the G20 Finance Ministers and Central Bank Governors on So-Called Stablecoins'. Available at: https://www.fatf-gafi.org/media/fatf/documents/recommendations/Virtual-Assets-FATF-Report-G20-So-Called-Stablecoins.pdf (accessed 17 October 2020)

10   Tran, H. and Matthews, B., 2020, 'China's Digital Currency Electronic Payment Project Reveals the Good and the Bad of Central Bank Digital Currencies – Atlantic Council', Atlantic Council. Available at: https://www.atlanticcouncil.org/blogs/new-atlanticist/chinas-digital-currency-electronic-payment-project-reveals-the-good-and-the-bad-of-central-bank-digital-currencies/ (accessed 17 October 2020)

Notes to Epilogue: Cryptopias                pages 153–162

1    Brown, G., 2020, 'Bitcoin: The UK and US Are Clamping
     Down on Crypto Trading – Here's Why It's Not Yet
     a Big Deal', *The Conversation*. Available at: https://
     theconversation.com/bitcoin-the-uk-and-us-are-clamping-
     down-on-crypto-trading-heres-why-its-not-yet-a-big-
     deal-147775 (accessed 17 October 2020)

2    Chainalysis (2020) *Investigating the Cryptocurrency
     Networks Funding Domestic Extremism* available at
     https://go.chainalysis.com/domestic-extremism-webinar-
     recording.html (accessed 1 February 2021)

3    Golumbia, D., *The Politics of Bitcoin: Software as right-
     wing extremism* (University of Minnesota Press, 2016)

4    Volpicelli, G., 2018, 'Steve Bannon Is Creating a
     "Deplorables" Cryptocurrency to Boost Global Populism',
     *WIRED UK*. Available at: https://www.wired.co.uk/article/
     steve-bannon-cryptocurrency-politics-token (accessed
     17 October 2020)

5    Volpicelli, G., 2018, 'Amir Fought Isis in Syria, Now He's
     Enlisting an Army of Hacker Monks to Save Bitcoin from

Itself', *WIRED UK*. Available at: https://www.wired.co.uk/
article/amir-taaki-dark-wallet-cryptocurrency-bitcoin-
revolution-catalonia (accessed 17 October 2020)

6   Buterin, V. and Weyl, G., 2018, 'Liberation Through
Radical Decentralization', *Medium*. Available at: https://
medium.com/@VitalikButerin/liberation-through-radical-
decentralization-22fc4bedc2ac (accessed 17 October 2020)

7   2019, 'Blockchain & Radicalxchange Communities: Better
Together' [image]. Available at: https://www.youtube.com/
watch?time_continue=89&v=ohL9258CEY4&feature=e
mb_logo (accessed 17 October 2020)

# Index

# WIRED Guides: the must-read series of WIRED books on the key trends and topics shaping our world.

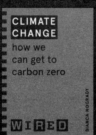

**CLIMATE CHANGE**

how we can get to carbon zero

WIRED

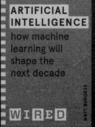

**ARTIFICIAL INTELLIGENCE**

how machine learning will shape the next decade

WIRED

**THE FUTURE OF MEDICINE**

how we will enjoy longer, healthier lives

WIRED

On sale March 2021

**THE FUTURE OF FOOD**

how to feed the planet without destroying it

WIRED

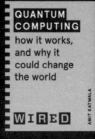

**QUANTUM COMPUTING**

how it works, and why it could change the world

WIRED

**CRYPTO CURRENCY**

how digital money could transform finance

WIRED

On sale from June 2021

# Subscribe to WIRED magazine

for the very best of what's coming next, in print and interactive digital editions.

The authority on the future of business, design, technology and culture

See the latest subscription offers at wired.co.uk

WIRED Consulting takes
the WIRED knowledge,
network and brand to our
clients, helping them
to drive innovation, shape
strategy and build their
voice on the trends
that are shaping our world.

# Insight into trends.
# Foresight for the future.
# Confidence on
# the path ahead.

Consulting@wired.co.uk

# Where the inspirational go to be inspired: top-level talks from key influencers across the WIRED network.

**WIRED Events.**

**Smarter.**
**Live.**
**Briefings.**
**Health.**

Visit wired.uk/events
for more on all our live
and virtual sessions